JEZEBELLION

THE WARRIOR'S GUIDE TO DEFEATING THE JEZEBEL SPIRIT

JEZEBELLION

THE WARRIOR'S GUIDE TO DEFEATING THE JEZEBEL SPIRIT

TIFFANY BUCKNER

Anointed Fire House™

Jezebellion:
The Warrior's Guide to Defeating the Jezebel Spirit
by Tiffany Buckner

www.tiffanybuckner.com
info@anointedfire.com

Published by Anointed Fire™ House
www.anointedfirehouse.com
Cover Design by Anointed Fire™ House
Author photograph by Dominique 'Chevon' Doyle
www.sochevon.com

ISBN-10: 0-9982507-5-9
ISBN-13: 978-0-9982507-5-5

I have tried to recreate events, locales and conversations from my memories of them. In order to maintain their anonymity in some instances, I have changed the names of individuals and places and I may have changed some identifying characteristics and details such as physical properties, occupations and places of residence.

Table of Contents

Foreword

I have had my share of run-ins with the Jezebel spirit. Many years ago, I nearly lost everything to this heinous spirit (including my life). While sitting in my room one night, I found myself suffocating under the clutches of fear, intimidation and control. This foul spirit has destroyed families, dismantled ministries and disintegrated churches all because of the simple fact that God's people have been ignorant to her evil agenda. Years ago, I learned how to break free from the grip of this evil (albeit unseen) spirit.

In this masterful work, Jezebellion, Tiffany Buckner snatches the mask off of this evil spirit. Through a careful application of God's Word and personal stories, Tiffany helps the reader to identify, resist and break free from the power of the Jezebel spirit. With the crystal clarity of a seasoned veteran and the humility of a woman of God, she does what many have not been able to do: expose the wicked agenda of Jezebel while leading the believer on a path to lasting freedom. As you read, pay close attention. Examine yourself and allow the Holy Spirit to do a deep work within your own heart and mind. You will be challenged, strengthened, convicted, encouraged and transformed.

Dr. Kynan Bridges
Bestselling Author, Unmasking The Accuser
Senior Pastor, Grace & Peace Global Fellowship, Inc.

Preface

When I wrote the *Jezebellion* series, my original plan was to write a single book. I thought the book would be around two hundred pages, but I was wrong. Before long, the book was over five hundred pages and because I know that a five hundred page book can be overwhelming to most readers, I decided to break the book up into two parts. Truthfully, none of my plans for *Jezebellion* seemed to pan out. It wasn't long before I realized that my plans were being overridden by God's plans. Of course, I finally decided to just do my part by writing the book and let God work out the details.

Volume One of the *Jezebellion* series is centered around identifying the Jezebel spirit. Even though a large number of Christians believe they know the traits of the Jezebel spirit, the truth is, they only know what can best be described as standard information. Standard information is what's generally taught and expounded upon in any given era based on a single source or a few sources. How so? Some of the pioneers of deliverance have come face-to-face with some of the most wicked principalities (like Jezebel), and they've written books and articles detailing what they learned while fighting these principalities. Even though their records are true and beneficial, a lot of people are now recording messages and writing both books and articles teaching about spirits that they have never warred with or spirits that they have very limited knowledge of. Because of this, they outsource their information, meaning, they take their knowledge from the pioneers who've been on the front-lines of the battlefield and have had to decapitate a few giants. In other words, they teach the same messages using different words. Now, don't get me wrong; there is nothing wrong with people 'resharing' information; however, where there is no confrontation, there is no new revelation. What this means is that we, as the body of Christ, have a tendency to feed on second-hand knowledge when, in truth, we need more revelation knowledge.

Of course, someone would come along and say, "Why do we need new knowledge when the old information is beneficial?" The short answer is: the Bible is beneficial for learning, but God still sends out prophets to be His mouthpieces. The long answer to this is: "*we know in part and we prophesy in part*" (1 Corinthians 13:9). When we stop seeking revelation knowledge, we start guarding certain access doors to our souls, all the while, leaving other access doors unguarded. Please understand that the enemy is crafty. If you expect him to send a blonde woman with blue eyes to deceive you, he'll send a brunet man with dark eyes in her place. This means that the old information is beneficial; however, we still need to seek new revelation because like viruses, demons tend to mutate or, better yet, change their methods of attack. That's because they aren't animals restricted to instinctual behaviors, nor are they robots that are pre-programmed to behave a certain way. They are a highly adaptable form of intelligence and they've managed to survive for billions of years through all of the climate changes, revolutions, and wars. Of course, the reason they've survived the natural elements is because they are spirit beings; however, there is an environment that is not conducive to their survival and that environment is a God-submitted heart.

One of my favorite scriptures is James 4:7, which reads, "*Submit yourselves therefore to God. Resist the devil, and he will flee from you.*" What this tells us is that by submitting to God and resisting the devil, we create environments within ourselves that the enemy cannot live in. As a matter of fact, the Bible tells us that he (the enemy) will flee from us whenever we become God-submitted vessels. Why does the Bible use the word "flee"? Simply put, the enemy is at war with us, therefore, he is either advancing towards us or retreating from us. The biblical reference to the word "flee" denotes victory on the part of the believer. It means that the believer is advancing against the enemy.

The point is ... we need new revelation to survive. For this reason, God has reserved many to be His prophets. Prophets aren't tape recorders. Prophets are God's mouthpieces; they are living books filled with the empty pages that God writes on whenever He wants to send forth new revelation, new knowledge, confirmation, warnings and the like. This means that God's prophets are 'Bibles' in the making. However, what God shares through His prophets today will never conflict with what He shared through the prophets of old. That's why a legalist is bound by a deaf and mute spirit. Even though they hear, they are deaf; and even though they speak, their words fall upon deaf ears. Legalists are souls who've opened their Bibles after the enemy has managed to close their hearts. What does this mean? They are wordsmiths who've mastered the cultural and historical definition of words, but cannot hear or understand the Word of God. This is simply because they have pre-determined within themselves that God no longer speaks when, of course, this is not true.

Demons have to adapt to many changes in order to survive. For example, the demon of rejection wasn't as prevalent amongst believers in the biblical times as it is today because back then, almost every home consisted of a father and a mother. Of course, the enemy has successfully waged war against God's definition of the word "family" and with each new norm that society accepts, new strongholds were developed by the kingdom of darkness to ensure the longevity of those norms. That's why we need new revelation, new strategies, and fresh-faced prophets who aren't bound by the cultural, traditional, or historical strongholds that the enemy has used to hinder many in the Church.

Jezebellion, Volume II is a book centered around both knowledge and warfare. It is an inside-view of Satan's favorite network of demons and how they operate. This isn't 'reshared' information; it is knowledge I've gained through my own personal dealings with the Jezebel principality, plus, the revelation that the Holy Spirit has given to me.

Introduction

The notorious Jezebel spirit is so wicked of a spirit that it is often referred to as the "bride of Satan." Crafty, manipulative, seductive and controlling, the Jezebel spirit has destroyed many good names, marriages, churches and lives. It prides itself on its ability to mask itself and deceive even the most astute believer.

Volume II of Jezebellion is a warfare and deliverance manual. This book is written to help you to better understand the kingdom of darkness; that way, you can effectively war against the Jezebel spirit, as well as any other demon that dares to rise against you. Volume I helped you to identify Jezebel's trademark behaviors, but Volume II is more-so a study of your enemy. Understand this: there is a difference between war and warfare and Satan gets the advantage over many believers because he engages them in warfare, while they try to engage him in war!

In this comprehensive guide, you will learn to strategize against the enemy who's been strategizing against you. You will learn how to take back your peace, joy and anything else Satan or his associate Jezebel has stolen from you!

CHAPTER 1

Unmasking Jezebel

In 2016, God birthed me into the ministry of deliverance. I hadn't had any formal teachings regarding deliverance; instead, a lot of what I learned about demonic spirits came from, of course, the Holy Spirit and from my many encounters with them. The Holy Spirit was and is my Teacher. At the same time, before I could even think about attempting to take anyone through deliverance, I first had to take myself through deliverance ... *repeatedly.*

Luke 6:42 (ESV): *How can you say to your brother, 'Brother, let me take out the speck that is in your eye,' when you yourself do not see the log that is in your own eye? You hypocrite, first take the log out of your own eye, and then you will see clearly to take out the speck that is in your brother's eye.*

By this time, I'd had countless encounters with the Jezebel spirit. As a matter of fact, God told me a few years earlier that He was going to use me to write a book about the Jezebel spirit. Every now and again, I would wonder when that time would come because I'd learned so much from encountering and wrestling with that spirit that I would always feel like I was ready to write the book. But I wasn't. The reason for this is ... I'd met Jezebel in a few of her forms, but there was much more to Jezebel than I understood. Even when I came in contact with people who had the Jezebel spirit, I would ignore God's voice *if* their traits did not line up with *my* definition of the Jezebel spirit. I looked for dominant control and sexual immorality, and while these are traits of the Jezebel spirit, there are more traits that many are unaware of.

Jezebels are often believed to be ungodly women who would stop at nothing to get what they want, but this is only a limited definition. The truth is ... the Jezebel spirit is a spirit, meaning, it does not possess a gender, even though most spirits are referred to using masculine verbiage. With that being said, the Jezebel spirit can inhabit a man, just as it can inhabit a woman. How do I know? I've met it a few times in men as well. Howbeit, the Jezebel spirit is more commonly found in women and there is a reason for this. The Jezebel spirit hates godly authority, so it prefers to dwell in women since God gave the husband the position of authority over his household. This includes his wife and children. In order for it to establish and strengthen itself, Jezebel first needs to operate in someone's legal authority. This is similar to what other demonic spirits do. They don't have earth-suits (bodies), and this renders them illegal in the realm of the earth, so they enter the bodies (legal vessels) of people and make their dwelling there. This is also similar to gang initiation. Gangs will often require their potential new members to commit a violent crime before they are accepted into the gang. This is called initiation. Demonic spirits have initiations too. For example, an Ahab is oftentimes nothing but a Jezebel in a training bra. The person is being trained to walk as a Jezebel. This initiation process is complete once the ahab'ed soul successfully manages to ahab a person of authority. In marriage, Jezebel needs to establish and strengthen herself by first getting the husband to relinquish his authority. She then has to operate in his authority, meaning, she begins to act as the head of the home. Why is this? Because God established a marital order that would ensure that He would remain as the supreme authority over that household. However, disorder removes God as the head or operable authority over a household so, in short, Jezebel needs to remove God to operate. By removing Christ (the head of the man) from the order that was instituted by God, Jezebel successfully manages to keep her lover from having the mind of Christ. This opens him up to one of the spirits in Jezebel's network called the spirit of mind control.

1 Corinthians 11:3 (ESV): *But I want you to understand that the head of every man is Christ, the head of a wife is her husband, and the head of Christ is God.*

As you can see, God has established an order that would ensure that He remains the head of every household. However, the Jezebel spirit cannot operate in a household where the order of God is faithfully carried out. So to establish itself and function, it first has to pervert (change the order around) so that the couple will operate in sin. Their disorderly marriage would then be rendered ungodly, making it an environment for Jezebel and other demonic spirits to thrive. For this reason, God told us to not be unequally yoked with unbelievers (2 Corinthians 6:14).

The Jezebel spirit is an illegal spirit that has no authority except the authority given to it by a believer. Think of it this way. If Ahab had not married Jezebel, she could not have come to Israel and started establishing laws. She would have been a trespasser; an illegal alien and as such, even the smallest of the Israelites would have had the legal authority to arrest (bind) her. However, when Ahab married her, he made the illegal woman a legal authority figure. Let's visit this from the spiritual side. It was many of our sins that allowed demonic spirits to enter us. Many of us were even once bound by genera-

tional demons that came in through our bloodline. Nevertheless, when we got saved, God canceled out the death in us that came in through our familial bloodlines with the blood of Christ Jesus. This is what rendered demonic spirits as illegal trespassers in our lives and that's why we have the legal right, authority and ability to cast them out of us. God is like the federal government of the United States. He has already established what is legal and illegal, but we are like governors. We get to determine what we deem legal or illegal in our own lives. This is what determines our states (conditions).
Luke 10:19 (ESV): *Behold, I have given you authority to tread on serpents and scorpions, and over all the power of the enemy, and nothing shall hurt you.*

Anytime we unequally yoke ourselves with unbelievers, we establish illegal unions where darkness attempts to merge with light. The problem with this is ... light has no communion (or fellowship) with darkness. This renders the relationship illegal and allows the Jezebel spirit to function in the darkness of that relationship. If the couple is married and one of the spouses fully submits himself or herself to God, that believer will cause the other spouse to be sanctified or made holy. This sounds great, but it is no easy feat.
1 Corinthians 7:13-16 (ESV): *If any woman has a husband who is an unbeliever, and he consents to live with*

her, she should not divorce him. For the unbelieving husband is made holy because of his wife, and the unbelieving wife is made holy because of her husband. Otherwise your children would be unclean, but as it is, they are holy. But if the unbelieving partner separates, let it be so. In such cases the brother or sister is not enslaved. God has called you to peace. For how do you know, wife, whether you will save your husband? Or how do you know, husband, whether you will save your wife?

Why is this no easy feat? The truth is ... if a believer is attracted to an unbeliever, that believer has something in common with the unbeliever. This is what brought them together in the first place. To submit fully to God, the believer has to die to self, go through deliverance (if needed) and become an entirely new creature in Christ Jesus. The problem with this is ... the unbeliever likely fell in love with the part of the believer that is now being commanded to die. For example, the believer may have been a wild, partying woman who loved porn. All of a sudden, she becomes a meek, God-fearing woman who walks in holiness. So, the unbeliever will feel as if he's lost his wife and he, along with the Jezebel spirit, will work tirelessly to resurrect the dead woman. One of Jezebel's most effective weapons is emotional pain, therefore, since the Jezebel spirit has access to the believer through the unbeliever, the Jezebel spirit will wreak havoc in the believer's life. The believer would essentially have to "get over herself," gain control over her emotions and serve God in the presence of a man who now sees her as a soft-spoken terrorist who's withholding his wife from him. Additionally, God won't force that man to serve Him. Instead, He gives the believing spouse a set of directions designed to help bring His light into their household; that way, the husband can and will be faced with the opportunity to choose God or choose the god of this world. In most cases, the unbeliever chooses to leave.

1 Peter 3:1-2 (ESV): *Likewise, wives, be subject to your own husbands, so that even if some do not obey the word, they may be won without a word by the conduct of their wives, when they see your respectful and pure conduct.*

1 Corinthians 7:15 (NLT): *But if the husband or wife who isn't a believer insists on leaving, let them go. In such cases the Christian husband or wife is no longer bound to the other, for God has called you to live in peace.*

The Jezebel spirit doesn't just thrive in marital relationships; it also thrives in church environments, business settings and any place order has been established but is not followed. What needs to be understood about this spirit is ... it craves authority and will always be found attempting to link itself with any person of authority or trying to climb the ladder of success to earn as much authority as possible.

People influenced by the Jezebel spirit tend to be underhanded, crafty, and unrepentant. They are self-absorbed, ambitious and oftentimes appear to be nurturing *(when they aren't trying to destroy you, of course)*. A few examples of Jezebels in action include, but definitely are not limited to:

- The workplace Jezebels who keep running to the manager's office to tell the manager about anyone they feel aren't doing their jobs or aren't doing their jobs properly. This is Jezebel's attempt to get authority over the people they are considered "equal to." They are trying to usurp the manager's authority. Jezebels don't see themselves as equal to anyone; they see themselves as the boss, even when they are not.
- The church Jezebel who somehow manages to get close to the pastor and starts monitoring his phone calls and visits. To get to the pastor, you must first go through Jezebel and tell her what you want. Jezebels like to sequester information; that way, they can have some leverage against a person should they not get what they want.
- The family Jezebel who insists on setting up every family reunion so she can establish the rules. She's the one who does almost all the work for

the family reunion and then, complains about having had to do all the work. She's also that family member who divides the family with gossip and slander, and then, in an attempt to appear honorable, will attempt to bring the family back together again ... on her terms.

There are a lot of misconceptions about the Jezebel spirit and it is our ignorance of this spirit that allows it to function in the church. Below are a few things I've learned about the Jezebel spirit through my own dealings with it and my own deliverance from it.

1. **Men can have Jezebels too:** I've met the Jezebel spirit in several men and when it enters a man, it robs the wife of her *legal* authority. What is her legal authority? Her legal authority is her right to think and behave as she pleases. God gives us free will; He allows us to choose between good and evil. However, when a man has the Jezebel spirit, he will oftentimes be insecure and emotionally unstable. He will have trust issues and those trust issues will eventually become control issues. He will monitor his wife's phone calls and associations, even attempting to tell her who she can or cannot be friends with. I once met that spirit in a man and he (the man) wanted to even

know his wife's thoughts. If he caught her dazing off into nothingness, he would ask her what she was thinking. If she refused to tell him, he'd punish her with the silent treatment, by leaving, or by escalating the event into a huge argument. Jezebellic men tend to be mentally and verbally abusive and most of them eventually escalate to physical abuse. They hate not being in full control of everything. They oftentimes believe themselves to be the victims of their wives' selfish ways, and because of this, they will oftentimes turn even the smallest infractions into huge arguments.

2. **Some married men are not married to their wives:** When a man's mother has the Jezebel spirit and he is operating as her Ahab, his marriage to his wife will not work unless he gets delivered and he maintains that deliverance. The reason for this is ... he has failed to cleave to his wife because he is still cleaving to his mother. This renders his house a house divided and of course, a house divided cannot stand (Mark 3:25). Because his mother is in charge, she is the head (authority) over his household and that's why she'll have the ability to determine if the couple has a good day or a bad day. She will control the direction of that marriage until it ends in

divorce or the husband repents of his sin, submits himself to God, and takes his authority back. In many cases, he will need to separate himself from his mother if she refuses to repent and get delivered. Please understand that Jezebel is married to Ahab, so anytime you come in contact with a person who has successfully ahab'ed another person, spiritually speaking, both parties are married. If you marry such a person, you will become the other woman or the other man.

3. **Jezebels can function as spirit husbands or wives:** Before I entered the ministry of deliverance, I'd watched a lot of videos about deliverance, with many of them being performed in Africa. I was fascinated with the many techniques used by both Americans and Africans to perform deliverance. At the same time, I heard about a demonic spirit called a spirit spouse (spirit husband or spirit wife). I listened to audio messages and read articles about the spirit spouses and amazingly enough, most of those teachings came from African ministries. I saw a few American ministers casting out spirit husbands and spirit wives, but not as much as the African ministries. One day, I realized that I needed to be delivered from a spirit husband because I'd dreamed that something was having sex with me. I coupled

that dream together with a few dreams I'd had, plus, the fact that I'd had two miscarriages. It wasn't long before I realized that I'd been bound by that thing for years. The messages all made sense to me so I prayed, went to the bathroom and God blessed me to take myself through deliverance (with His finger, of course). Eventually, I entered the ministry of deliverance and started performing mass deliverance sessions via my Friday night conference calls. I would always call out the spirit husbands (since my calls consist of 98-99 percent women) and there would always be a huge manifestation. I could hear women vomiting, crying, and demons begging over the line. Eventually, God began to deal with me about the Jezebel-Ahab relationship and what I've discovered is that a spirit husband or spirit wife is sometimes nothing but the infamous Jezebel and Ahab spirits. Remember, Jezebel is married to Ahab. God reminded me of what I used to say of and feel about my ex-husband, Roger, and his relative, Mara. I would always say that I believed the two of them were married because she'd exhibited a lot of unnatural behaviors toward him and a lot of hatred and jealousy towards me. At the same time, he felt obligated to satisfy her, even if that meant disappointing me. When we visited her (before I stopped dealing with her), she would beat incessantly on the bedroom door that we were sleeping in. When we opened the door, she would pretend to be looking for silly things like batteries or her shoes (even though that wasn't her bedroom). Sometimes, she would not say what she was looking for; she'd just start looking under the bed, in the closet and around the room. After that, she would ask Roger what we were doing and, of course, this was extremely strange. She would also keep calling him out the room if he was spending time with me. She always felt the need to compete with me and I truly felt like the other woman. When my mother met Roger and we stayed at her house a few weeks, she immediately noticed how unnatural his relationship was with Mara because Mara kept calling her house for him. He'd disappear into another room and talk with her for hours; this was a daily occurrence. Because of this, my mother called me to another room and asked me if I was *sure* Mara has related to him. They were definitely related, but what I came to soon discover was ... what was in Mara was married to what was in Roger and I was the *other woman* after all! This is also true, for example, if you see a mother who treats her son as if he is her husband or a father who treats his daughter as if she is his wife. The truth of the matter is ... what's in operation is, of course, the Jezebel-Ahab alliance and Jezebel is married to Ahab! If you get involved with an Ahab, you will be seen by Jezebel as the other woman or the other man. Additionally, Jezebel will operate as a spirit wife and Ahab will operate as a spirit husband.

4. **Not all African American women are Jezebels and not all Caucasian Women are Ahabs:** As an African American woman, I am aware of the many assumptions that some races have regarding Africans and African Americans. African and African American women are often believed to be dominant and controlling and this is *not* true. Caucasian women are believed to be easily controlled and this is *not* true. There are some dominant and controlling African and African American women out there, just like there are some dominant and controlling Caucasian women out there. Many African and African American women are passive, but the media likes to portray the idea that we are naturally dominant and truthfully, this is false advertising. In *every* race, there are dominant women, just as there are passive women. For example, I was once married to an African man and my experience with him was horrible,

however, I don't assume that everyone from his country is like him or Mara. As a matter of fact, while married to him, I met many Africans from numerous countries, including his country, and this helped me to realize that a lot of what I was enduring with him and Mara was not cultural, nor was it normal. Promoting the idea that one race has more Jezebels in it promotes stereotypes, racism and allows the Jezebel spirit to slither by undetected. Sometimes, generalization is just a lazy man's attempt to appear educated.

5. **Sometimes, race baiting is Jezebel's attempt to find an Ahab or Ahab's attempt to find a Jezebel:** In the African American community, it is not uncommon to hear a man say that he is not going to date or marry African American women ... *anymore*. Now, don't get me wrong, there is *nothing* wrong with interracial courtship and marriage *at all*, however, when a man *specifically* singles out a race, it is likely because he has a hidden agenda or a misconception about that race. Most of the men who say this have been hurt and are bitter towards women *as a whole*, but because they've only dated African American women, they will assume that the problem is in the African American race. In most cases, men like this have the notorious Jezebel spirit and

what they are saying is that they've been unsuccessful in their attempts to ahab the women they've courted or married. *Please note again that not all African American women are dominant; there are just as many (or more) passive African American women as there are dominant ones. Some men are attracted to dominant women because they represent a challenge to them. Then again, some of those men are looking for women to act as their mothers. When they are unsuccessful at conquering those women and when their relationships fail, they become even more bitter than they were when they entered those relationships. They then blame it on the race and the gender, but not their choices or their own attitudes.* This means that they have not and will not accept responsibility for their own actions. This is the Jezebel spirit in full effect! Because they lack understanding, they think that non-black women are passive and easier to control and this is *not* true. For this reason, they are very strategic in their searches for the perfect non-black woman. Men like this will find a crowd of non-black women and choose the shyest, most insecure woman in that crowd and then, rush the relationship so they can hurry up and create a soul tie with her. *Remember, Jezebel likes to create soul ties and she likes to create them fast.* After that, they will begin to abuse, mistreat and control the women *if allowed.* Of course, it goes without saying that not all African American men who are attracted to non-black women are Jezebels. Some are decent men who simply have their own preferences *(and there's nothing wrong with that)*, however, anytime you hear a man *specifically* and *bitterly* write off a race, it is likely because he has been hurt and he has been unsuccessful at controlling the women of that race. When a man who has the Jezebel spirit successfully marries a non-black woman and finds he cannot control her, he will then start speaking bitterly towards the female gender as a whole. *Most of us have witnessed this a few times.* Such men often use derogatory terms when referring to women. The same is true for a non-black man, for example, who assumes that all African American women are dominant. Because of this, he seeks a dominant, African American woman and when he finds one, he is quick to marry her. Such a man is bound by the Ahab spirit *because he sought a dominant woman* to take the headship position; it didn't matter if he sought that woman in his own race or another race. Anytime a man seeks to be controlled, it is because he is perverted and has the

Ahab spirit.

6. **Jezebels are created in pain, trained in pain and sent out in pain:** Their goal is to kill the prophets, steal from the people of God and destroy God's works in the earth. They work tirelessly to create duplicates of themselves. The Jezebel spirit is like a virus. It is infectious and easily transferred. That's why Jezebels are attracted to people who are hurting. They will take those people under their broken wings and try to open them up to receive the Jezebel spirit. For example, if a woman is suffering from a recent breakup and Jezebel spots her, Jezebel will attempt to console her. She will offer her good *and* ungodly advice (the purpose of the good advice is to keep her from blowing her religious cover). She may even offer her a place to stay if she needs one and help her to feel stable again, but this is not free. Jezebel is working hard to make that woman feel obligated to her; that way, she can use what she's done for her to control her. She will also use that opportunity to speak word curses or perform witchcraft over the woman's estranged lover. This is because when the Jezebel spirit is in a woman, it will often promote the hatred of men and the belief that all men are promiscuous, when this is not true. Of course, these

beliefs were established in pain and reaffirmed by her repeated bad choices with men. Such a woman has a habit of choosing ungodly men, and then, complaining about them behaving in ungodly ways.

7. **Jezebels are repeatedly broken to maintain their hard hearts:** One of the things I've noticed about people who have the Jezebel spirit is that they are always being attacked and broken by the enemy. The reason for this is because sometimes, they will start to soften up (especially if they're being ministered to or someone has been sharing God's love with them). When Jezebels get too soft, Satan uses someone in their immediate circle to hurt them all over again. This is to reestablish and reaffirm their beliefs that their evil ways, insecurities and hatred for authority has been beneficial to them. For example, let's say a man who has the Jezebel spirit has been repeatedly hurt by women, but one day, he meets a loving woman who seems to be determined to win him over to the Lord. Despite his many tantrums and his controlling ways, his new love interest sticks around and keeps praying for him. Slowly, but surely, his heart begins to soften up and he finds himself wanting to go to church more. The Jezebel spirit will see this and look for a way to

break him all over again. For example, his new love interest may have been sent by the enemy to deceive the man and then, break his heart. Then again, she may be a good woman, but she hasn't exactly told her ex to stop contacting her. One day, she receives a text message from her ex. The only thing he says is, "Hello. I still can't get you out of my mind." Her new love interest happens to be in the living room with her phone while she's in the kitchen preparing a meal. He opens her text messages and sees the text. From there, his heart is broken all over again and the Jezebel spirit will begin to reaffirm his dark beliefs. The Jezebel spirit will never allow its host to experience true happiness.

8. **The Jezebel spirit is the same personality the world is now identifying as the narcissist.** The Mayo Clinic lists the following symptoms of narcissism: grandiosity, callous and unemotional traits, disregard for others' feelings, excessive need for admiration, receptor antagonist, or social isolation. In the church, we know these to be the traits of the Jezebel spirit, but the world is now identifying certain demonic personalities and attempting to diagnose and treat them. Of course, demons cannot be treated; they have to be cast out!

9. **Jezebel is known as the "queen of heaven."** Catholics also identify the virgin Mary as the "queen of heaven." This is no coincidence. The truth is ... a Roman emperor by the name of Constantine tried to Christianize the Romans, but they were resistant, so he decided to compromise with them. He allowed them to bring in many of their pagan beliefs and gods (demons) and he simply changed the names of their gods (demons) to Christian names. This was the start of the Roman Catholic church, from which, all Christian churches today initially stemmed. Mary suddenly became "the queen of heaven" and people were allowed to start worshiping her. Of course, we know that Mary was never supposed to be worshiped. When Mary is lifted up as an idol, the Jezebel spirit will always thrive because by worshiping "the queen of heaven," many people don't realize they're actually worshiping Jezebel.
10. **Jezebels cause droughts:** Anytime you go under the covering of a Jezebel ministry or a Jezebel-run establishment, you will experience a drought in your life. The reason for this is because Baal (the demon who Jezebel worshiped) was also referred to as "the lord of rain." For this reason, God did not allow it to rain in Israel for

three and a half years. This was to prove that Baal did not control the weather. After Elijah confronted Ahab and God proved Himself to be the only true and living God by raining down fire on Elijah's offering, the people repented and announced that YAHWEH is God. This means they rejected Baal and turned their hearts back to God. Not long after that, God allowed the rain to pour yet again. Anytime you submit yourself to Jezebel, there will be a drought in your life and that drought will end when you repent, renounce Baal and announce that YAHWEH is God.

11. **Elijah was the one who prayed for the drought.** James 5:17-18 (ESV) reads, *"Elijah was a man with a nature like ours, and he prayed fervently that it might not rain, and for three years and six months it did not rain on the earth. Then he prayed again, and heaven gave rain, and the earth bore its fruit."* Elijah wanted to prove that Baal was not god once and for all. What does this mean for the true prophets of God? It means that we have the power and the authority to control the weather in Jezebel and Ahab's lives if we'll only trust God and pray. Sometimes, we complain about Jezebel-run ministries and Jezebel-infected ministers, when we have the authority to shut down their ministries. Jezebel-led ministries

thrive today because we, as the church, have yet to cut off their lights or shut off their water!

12. **The Jezebel spirit had shown up before Jezebel, the woman, was born and after she died:** Jezebel is the same spirit that attacked Samson through Delilah (there is also a seductive spirit called the Delilah spirit as well). It manipulated Samson into telling Delilah the secret of his strength, and once Samson revealed this secret, Delilah turned him over to his enemies. This was undoubtedly the Jezebel spirit in action. It is the same spirit that led Solomon astray, causing him to worship other deities. It is the same spirit that kept Vashti from going before the king when called. It was the same spirit that caused Herodias to request the head of John, the Baptist, on a platter. It is the same spirit that provoked and led the Pharisees. Of course, it is the same spirit that led Queen Athaliah. We often call out different demonic spirits in the deliverance arena and, of course, the Jezebel spirit often comes with a network of other spirits, but the truth is ... the Jezebel spirit is and has always been Satan's most used and most effective demon to date.

We must understand that Jezebel wears many masks and if we are to effectively fight and overcome that principality, we need to understand when we are being confronted by it. We have to also understand what spirits are normally a part of its network; that way, we don't cast out Jezebel but leave its buddies behind. When this happens, the demons that were *not* cast out will always reopen the door to the demon that was cast out and it'll bring back seven spirits more wicked than itself.

Matthew 12:43-45 (ESV): *"When the unclean spirit has gone out of a person, it passes through waterless places seeking rest, but finds none. Then it says, 'I will return to my house from which I came.' And when it comes, it finds the house empty, swept, and put in order. Then it goes and brings with it seven other spirits more evil than itself, and they enter and dwell there, and the last state of that person is worse than the first. So also will it be with this evil generation."*

CHAPTER 2

Breaking Up with Jezebel

One of the keys to ending a relationship is first acknowledging that there is a relationship. This doesn't mean that you are somehow entangled in a *romantic* relationship with Jezebel; it means that you have a relationship with Jezebel that needs to end once and for all. One of the reasons people have trouble freeing themselves from Jezebel's fangs is because people generally have a hard time acknowledging their own errors. How is this related to breaking up with Jezebel? Every person that Jezebel is soul-tied to has been tolerating Jezebel and is, therefore, not an innocent victim of Jezebel's crimes against them. For example, there was a time when I saw myself as a victim. When I was in that mindset, I focused on the person who had the Jezebel spirit, but I did not focus on the spirit itself.

Ephesians 6:12 (ESV): *For we do not wrestle against flesh and blood, but against the rulers, against the authorities, against the cosmic powers over this present darkness, against the spiritual forces of evil in the heavenly places.* Because I focused on individual personali ties, rather than the spirit itself, I found myself entangled in Jezebel's web again and again. Each time, I would get away from one person who had the Jezebel spirit, I'd find myself befriending another person who had that spirit. Consequentially, I found myself getting angry with people, and I would end my relationship with people, but not with Jezebel. After all, I didn't realize that I had a relationship with a demonic spirit that would continue until I ended it.

There is a difference between the Jezebel personality versus the Jezebel spirit. What is the difference? Understand this: the word "personality" derives from the word "person." The suffix "ality" comes from the word "actual" and it means "the state of." Therefore, the word "personality" means "the state of the person." It is the characteristics that distinguish each person's individual state. So, the Jezebel personality references a merging of each individual's personality with the traits of the Jezebel spirit. The Jezebel spirit itself has characteristics that are unmistakable, even when they merge with the personalities of human beings. So, you can hide in caves and run away from certain personality types, but until you end your relationship with Jezebel, that spirit is going to keep coming after you. It's going to find another person whom it has access to and send that person into your life. When you tire of that person's ways and end your relationship with that person, Jezebel will get behind the "will" of another person and send them into your life. This cycle will not end until you break it. Why is this? As long as you're operating as an ahab, Jezebel sees you as "home" and demons will always return to the place that they call "home."

One thing you'll discover is when you break up with the Jezebel spirit, you won't be able to tolerate its characteristics, nor will you be able to tolerate the Jezebel personality. When I started binding that spirit, severing all ungodly soul ties that I was a part of, and actively warring against that spirit, I could no longer tolerate some of the people I'd allowed into my life. I saw pride for what it is and it became detestable to me. I could no longer stomach listening to people talking about themselves for hours on end. I could no longer watch Jezebel play the innocent victim after she attacked folks in the name of being righteous. The reason for this is ... when I stopped tolerating Jezebel, I could no longer tolerate folks who had the Jezebel spirit.

Now, don't get me wrong ... sometimes, we will come in contact with nice, well-meaning folks who have simply inherited the Jezebel spirit. Those folks may genuinely love God and want to serve Him, but what I've found is this: even if the Jezebel spirit is inherited, any person bound by it can be free from it *if they want* to be free. All too often, we help people make excuses for being self-centered and venomous. I had to stop making excuses for the Jezebel personality and simply show folks the way to freedom. If they don't want to be free, you shouldn't tolerate them in hopes that someday, they'll change their minds. In my own personal experiences with Jezebel, what I've found is that many people who have the Jezebel spirit love being the way that they are. They don't want to change. You'll find that religious Jezebels want the benefits of Kingdom living, without the sacrifices. They don't want to give up being controlling, manipulative, seductive or any trait they feel has benefited them in their lives.

Breaking up with the Jezebel spirit is a lot easier than breaking up with the Jezebel personality. Why is this? Because when you break up with that spirit, you are ending your dealing with that spirit once and for all. This does not mean that the Jezebel spirit won't pursue you, attack you or attempt to "expose" you, but it does mean that you won't tolerate Jezebel anymore. In other words, you won't be personally entangled with someone who has that spirit for too long. Once you see its trademark behaviors, you'll know what to do.

What if you've been tolerating Jezebel? How do you rid

your life of that wicked demon?

Focus on the Demon, Not the Person

First and foremost, make sure that you're focused on the demon and not the person who has the demon. People often pose the wrong questions and because of this, they end up getting the answers they want, but not the answers they need. For example, people often ask God to show them how to get away from certain people. They pray away other people and consequentially, they keep dealing with the same demon in different people. What has to happen is ... you have to end your relationship with the Jezebel spirit, meaning, you have to be delivered from the spirit that's attracting Jezebel to you. Now, before we move forward, let's get one thing clear. If God has anointed you as a prophet of His, you will have a lifelong war with Jezebel. That demon will seek to attack and destroy you but, of course, God will protect you. However, the goal of deliverance is to ensure that you are not bound by any demonic spirits, including the ones that are in Jezebel's network. It is also to ensure that you are not attacked from within. So, to break up with Jezebel, you need to break up with whatever it is that Jezebel is attracted to. This means that if you've been operating under the Ahab spirit, you will need to renounce that spirit, cast it into the abyss, and start walking boldly in your God-given authority.

Walk in the Authority God Gave You

You have to walk in your God-given authority consistently and stop apologizing for being who God has designed you to be. One of the trademarks of the Ahab spirit is that people who have it are afraid to be themselves and are always trying to downplay who they are in order to make others feel better about themselves.

Stop Tolerating Jezebel

Next, you have to stop tolerating Jezebel. The way you do this is by telling Jezebel the truth. Don't let her complain in your ears anymore. When someone with the Jezebel spirit calls you and starts complaining, stop them in the middle of their rant and remind them of how good God is. Tell them to focus on all the good things that God has done for them, instead of focusing on all the bad things that they may be facing. Don't let them finish dumping on you; stop them mid-conversation, otherwise, they'll learn to call you up, rant about whatever it is they want to rant about, and then, get off the phone before you rebuke them. In other words, stop being Jezebel's toilet.

Don't Let Jezebel Gossip in Your Ears

Jezebels love gossip and slander and they will find creative ways to talk about others, even to their pastors. They'll disguise their words as warnings or words spoken out of concern when, in truth, they like to sow discord by sowing negative seeds. Don't let her talk about people to you anymore. Jezebels tend to be narcissistic and egotistical and, for this reason, they like to focus on the flaws of others. They are pharisaic in nature, always boasting on their own strengths and works, all the while, pointing out the weaknesses and failures of others. They love to catch people in error; that way, they can point out facts about the person before they attempt to expose them.

Luke 18:9-14 (ESV): *He also told this parable to some who trusted in themselves that they were righteous, and treated others with contempt: "Two men went up into the temple to pray, one a Pharisee and the other a tax collector. The Pharisee, standing by himself, prayed thus: 'God, I thank you that I am not like other men, extortioners, unjust, adulterers, or even like this tax collector. I fast twice a week; I give tithes of all that I get.' But the tax collector, standing far off, would not even lift up his eyes to heaven, but beat his breast, saying, 'God, be merciful to me, a sinner!' I tell you, this man went down to his house justified, rather than the other. For everyone who exalts himself will be humbled, but the one who humbles himself will be exalted."*

Don't Let Her Worship Herself in Your Ears

Don't let her talk for hours about herself anymore. Don't

let her play the victim anymore. Start telling her the truth about herself. You don't have to be rude with it. To Jezebel, the truth told in love is still offensive. Pay attention. When Jezebel calls you over the phone, she will ask you about your day. She'll start off with, "How was your day, man of God?" or "How are you doing, woman of God?" Once you finish answering her question, Jezebel will take over the call. In her attempt to not appear selfish, she gave you a full minute to talk about yourself, but after that, your purpose is to sit there and listen to Jezebel talk about herself, her day, her enemies, her thoughts and so on. Stop her. Don't sit there for thirty minutes or more listening to Jezebel rant about her day or worship herself. One of the most effective ways to do this is by cutting her off and correcting her or by changing the topic of the conversation (which is usually herself). Once I suspected that a woman I was associating with had the Jezebel spirit, I started toying with that spirit. When she would go on and on about herself, I'd wait for her to breathe and I'd jump in and start talking about something else. She'd get annoyed and try to redirect the conversation back to herself, but every time she did, I'd let her talk for a few minutes, and then, I'd redirect the conversation again. Of course, I'd respond to whatever she was talking about, but then, I'd change the subject and start talking about God. She'd get annoyed and suddenly someone in the background would grab her attention. She would get off the phone with me and she'd call me back later on to talk about herself some more. Of course, I was in error because I was tolerating that spirit in her, but once God confirmed once and for all that she indeed had the Jezebel spirit, I stopped toying with that spirit in her and I started rebuking it. Once Jezebel knew that her cover was blown, she could not and would not tolerate me any further.

Note: Don't overdo it. We all have our fair share of "selfish" days, especially when we're excited, angry or sad. However, Jezebel's selfish days outweigh her selfless days, so if you know that it is the pattern of a person to call and talk incessantly about themselves, stop them. But if a person is just having a bad day or is excited about something, don't assume they have the Jezebel spirit and then, proceed to handle them as such.

Don't be a Yes Man or a Yes Woman

Jezebel hates truth. She will almost always cast herself as the victim, even when she is the one who has clearly initiated an argument, fight, or an attack. Don't agree with Jezebel. Tell her that she's wrong when you see that she's in error. Here's what will happen when you do this. Jezebels normally have other friends, all of which are "yes" men and women. She will call them to talk about you and one of those friends will say something so interesting to her that she'll feel the need to say it to you. She'll likely call and try to reengage you in that conversation, and from there, she will find some type of way of accuse you of wrongdoing or she'll point out one of your flaws. Correct her with the Word of God. Don't argue in the flesh and don't use human reasoning. Instead, while she's talking, let the Holy Spirit give you the right scriptures to address her with. Remember, when Jesus was being tempted by Satan, He did not respond to him using human reasoning. He used the Word against him. Jezebel will likely call you and start quoting scriptures. Be ready. Come back at her with the Word of God in love. Once cornered, Jezebel will do the very same thing that Satan did when he could not use the scriptures to deceive the Lord. She will expose the wickedness of her heart and begin to speak evil. One of the reasons you should never have a flesh-to-flesh reasoning session with someone who has the Jezebel spirit is ... they will find error in your flesh and they will twist your words until you get upset. This is very similar to what demons do when a person is going through deliverance. They will try to upset the deliverance minister and get the minister to focus on the flesh of the person, instead of them. For example, they may cause the person to spit on the minister or mock the man or woman of God. When they do this, they are simply trying to distract the minister with the person's flesh. Jezebels do this in conversation. They want you to have a flesh-to-flesh conversation with them so that they can upset you, humiliate you or threaten you. If they get you in your flesh, they will record you or three-way someone else into the conversation secretly so that they can hear you reacting in an ungodly way. Nevertheless, anytime you come after a spirit with the Word of God, it will take off its mask and begin to curse at you.

Break Up with Jezebel Today

One of the most common questions people ask when referencing the Jezebel spirit is, "How do I end a friendship with someone who has the Jezebel spirit without coming off as mean?" One response I often give is ... there is no nice way to break up with a witch. It doesn't matter how nice you are, if you tell someone that you don't want to deal with them anymore, they will not focus on your loving tone or your long endearing farewell speech. All they will hear is that you don't want to deal with them anymore. Remember, you're not breaking up with people; you are breaking up with the demon that's in the people. With that being said, if a person does not want to be free from the Jezebel spirit or any other unclean spirit, you have to separate yourself from that person as well. *Of course, this does not include spouses or young children.*

I used to pray and ask the Lord to shut the door between me and anyone I saw the Jezebel personality resonating through. Unbeknownst to me, I was praying the wrong prayer. What I should have asked the Lord was to deliver me from every unclean spirit that was operating in me. By divorcing the Ahab spirit, I was simultaneously divorcing the Jezebel spirit. This means that I did not have to fast for 47 days or speak in tongues for 12 hours to drive Jezebel out of my life. All I had to do was go through deliverance myself and begin to walk in the authority that Christ Jesus availed to me. After that, I had to stop tolerating Jezebel, meaning, I stopped calling good "bad" and I stopped calling bad "good." When someone sinned against God, I corrected them in love *and* in authority, and if they refused to repent, I separated myself from them. I stopped acting like I couldn't see Jezebel performing her witchcraft or setting the stage for another one of her performances. I started acting like Elijah and I confronted the Ahab in me. I started acting like Micaiah and I prophesied to the Ahab that was operating in me. After that, I took it to war and pierced it with the sword of the Spirit. After I was delivered from the Ahab spirit, I started acting like Jehu and I confronted Jezebel in her high place (pride). Simply put, I broke up with Jezebel by sending her husband to the abyss and by confronting her. Then, I took it a step further. The Lord wanted to use me in deliverance ministry and I answered the call on my life. Using the finger of God, I started casting the Jezebel spirit out of others, along with other demonic spirits. Truthfully, when I entered the ministry of deliverance, there was no way that I could tolerate Jezebel anymore because I could no longer deny what I was seeing. I had to call Jezebel by her actual name and stop pretending that I didn't see her.

To break up with Jezebel, you have to break up with whomever Jezebel is married or connected to. At the same time, don't soul tie yourself to folks who are soul tied to Jezebel. Jezebel loves soul ties and if she can't directly soul-tie herself to you, she will try to send people into your life who she has soul ties with. She will then proceed to use them as monitoring spirits. When someone in your life is tolerating Jezebel, correct them in love, but if they do not stop tolerating Jezebel, you need to distance yourself from them. Think of it this way. If you broke up with a person and you genuinely wanted to be free from that person, chances are, you will stop dealing with any mutual friends that you have with that person. Why is this? Because, like God, you understand the heart of loyalty.

Matthew 6:24 (ESV): *No one can serve two masters, for either he will hate the one and love the other, or he will be devoted to the one and despise the other.*

2 Corinthians 6:14 (ESV): *Do not be unequally yoked with unbelievers. For what partnership has righteousness with lawlessness? Or what fellowship has light with darkness?*
Proverbs 13:20 (ESV): *Whoever walks with the wise becomes wise, but the companion of fools will suffer harm.*

I'm not telling you to judge anyone who's connected to Jezebel, but you do need to beware of them because there's something in them that allows Jezebel to operate without disruption in their lives. Minister to them, pray for them, but don't get too personal with them. As always, be led by the Holy Spirit.

Cast Jezebel out of your life once and for all. Break up with that wicked spirit by receiving deliverance yourself and then, stop tolerating it!

CHAPTER 3

Jezebel's Web

It goes without saying that Jezebel is a deceptive spirit and it prides itself on deceiving the saints of God. The Jezebel spirit thrives on the lack of knowledge that most people have regarding it. For example, it is not uncommon to see someone with a Jezebel spirit speaking with a group of believers about the traits and characteristics of the Jezebel spirit. What's funny is ... when this happens, people will intentionally avoid listing the traits that manifest through themselves, but will list the characteristics that they've witnessed manifesting through others. For example, a passive, soft-spoken Jezebel will point out the more dominant, controlling Jezebels and their ways, but will not list her own. A seductive Jezebel will point out the legalistic ways of an abstinent, religious Jezebel who follows the law to the letter. Here's the thing: the kingdom of darkness is not divided against itself. What's happening here is ... you are witnessing the territorial nature of a Jezebel. The demons in each person are just competing for the assignment, but ultimately, they are all on one accord. They want to destroy whatever person, family, ministry or group that they're competing over.

The Jezebel spirit spins an intricate web of deceit using lies, flattery and religion to capture its prey. A very cunning spirit, it relies on a person's lack of knowledge, coupled with an unmet desire in any given area to ensnare that person. All too often, believers find themselves idolizing something or someone, and when this happens, Jezebel will move in for the kill. Just like a spider, it must weave a strong web (stronghold) and rush to any prey that gets caught up in that web if it wants to ensure success.

Most Jezebels are religious and will always default to religion when cornered. Please understand that there is a difference between religiousness versus righteousness. A religious person follows a set of rules that were either imposed by their religion or self-imposed because of lack of knowledge, but they have no true heart for God. Someone who is righteous has received the Word of God and believes the Word of God.

A religious person is more concerned about what others think of them than what God says about them. Their religion is their god and they will often follow it to the letter. A righteous person is more concerned about what

God says of them than what people think about them. JEHOVAH is our God, and for this reason, a righteous person moves, behaves and reasons differently than a religious person. Jezebels are always religious, even when they are seated in churches where righteousness is promoted. The reason for this is ... Jezebel's assignment is to capture true believers (especially prophets) and lead them into their religious webs of deception. To do this, Jezebels first need to get others to believe that they are either righteous, loving, or needed. They have to get others to believe that they have their best interest in mind. This is a part of their web of deceit.

The Jezebel spirit spins many webs and each web has a different function, depending on Jezebel's agenda. Some of the various agendas of the Jezebel spirit include, but are not limited to:

- Recruiting and training other Jezebels
- Gathering Ahabs
- Gathering followers for themselves
- Destroying godly businesses
- Destroying families
- Destroying marriages
- Destroying churches and prophets

Recruiting and Training Other Jezebels

When I was a preteen, my family moved to some new

apartments and even though I wasn't excited about the move, like any other preteen, I was excited about the opportunity to meet new people ... *namely boys.* We moved into an apartment community and almost immediately, the neighborhood boys took notice of me. *That's because I was a new young woman in their community and I didn't know their reputations.* One of the first things we noticed was that my bedroom window had a black substance on it that we immediately identified as tar. Someone had tarred the window shut to keep it from opening. Of course, we lived in a downstairs apartment, so we reasoned that the culprit behind the tarring was a desperate father who was trying to either keep his daughter from sneaking out the window or keep some young boy from sneaking in the window. Of course, that room ended up becoming my room. *I think my dad suggested it.*

The first few days in the new apartment were fun for me. My parents had to work, but had somehow managed to unpack everything and put it away. A few teenage boys from the neighborhood befriended my brother and were asking him a lot of questions about me. They would stand outside while he came inside to relay the questions to me. Not long after that, they started knocking on the living room window and asking my brother for my response. When they saw me in the house, they kept asking me to come to the window. I was only twelve or thirteen years old, so I would giggle but I wouldn't come outside.

The first day that this happened, my mom came home and confronted me. A woman living in the community had called her at work and told her about the boys hanging around the apartment because of me. She told my mother that the guys had been knocking on the window and the door, and she went on to tell my mother how bad this looked. So, it goes without saying that my mom rebuked me and demanded that I put a stop to the boys' behavior. The problem was ... I didn't know how to do this, so I reasoned within myself that I would not come to the window. The next day, my mother came home from work (I think she was on her break) and started rebuking me, all the while, grabbing my arm so she could whoop me. She told me what the woman said as she prepared to whoop me. Mrs. Cox (the woman who'd called my mother) claimed that I'd lifted up my bedroom window and let some of the boys come in through my window. This was all a lie. Sure enough, the guys had come by the apartment and knocked on the living room window, but I did not let them in. I don't remember them knocking on my bedroom window, however. As a matter of fact, I don't even think I came to the window to address them because I'd already been threatened and I knew my mom wasn't the type of person to make idle threats. Nevertheless, there I stood, trying to tell the truth to my mother, but she wouldn't hear it. *She couldn't hear it.* She'd fallen into Jezebel's web because she had always been the type of person to believe any and everyone who was older than herself. She always honored her elders with "ma'am" or "sir" and she took everything they said at face value. That's how she was raised. At the same time, my mother was shy and always worried about what folks thought of her. She hated that we were already drawing negative attention to ourselves (and her), so she felt like she had to do something to not only stop the guys from coming to our apartment, but she wanted to be able to respond to Mrs. Cox when she called back. She wanted to show Mrs. Cox that she not only believed her, but she'd taken action. That was the day that I got the beating of my life. I was hurt and angry because the whooping wasn't justified. Mrs. Cox had lied on me, but I couldn't convince my mom of this truth because I was a child and Mrs. Cox was an older woman, so in my mom's mind, I was automatically the liar. At the same time, this was one of the many times I'd been lied on by an adult and not just any adult, but in this particular case, a somewhat elderly woman (I think she was around 55 years old). I was coming to see the world for what it was and not the fairy tale I once thought it to be.

Later that evening, my dad came home in a good mood, but he was greeted by the obvious tension in the house. My mom told him what Mrs. Cox said and she told him that she'd whooped me. *I think she wanted him to whoop me as well.* That's when my dad remembered something that I should have remembered while pleading my case. He told my mom, "That's impossible. Remember, Tiffany's window is tarred down. There's no way she could have opened it. I can't even open it." At that moment, I began to sob and I screamed to my mother, "I told you she was lying on me!" I finally felt like someone of authority believed me because my mom wouldn't listen to me. I was a young woman, but I got a chance to see how powerful and influential the Jezebel spirit can be. Of course, I didn't know what the Jezebel spirit was back then, but again, when I came to Christ and started looking back over my life, I was able to identify the many encounters I'd had with Jezebel as a young woman.

My mom was always in the clutches of some Jezebel because she was extremely passive and did not know how to say no to people. She hated disappointing people, so regardless of how she felt, she was always busy doing something for somebody. At the same time, my dad hated disappointing her, so as I grew up, I became defensive in an attempt to protect myself. I was molested a lot because our home was open to any family member or family friend who needed somewhere to stay. Needless to say, I found myself living with Jezebels who preyed on my mother's fear of saying no and my father's fear of upsetting my mother. Of course, this was the Ahab spirit in operation and that's how I ended up with that spirit. I didn't' realize it then, but an Ahab is oftentimes nothing but a Jezebel in training.

When I was a young woman, I manifested all of the trademarked behaviors of the Jezebel spirit. I was controlling, seductive, promiscuous and I had a serious problem with men. What I later came to realize was that my childhood was nothing but what I now call Jezebel University ... the place where Jezebels are taught to be Jezebels.

Even as a child, I witnessed some of my friends being trained by the Jezebel spirit through molestation, parental rejection and dysfunction. What I've come to learn is that Jezebels are often created in pain and in desperation. You see, in order to establish itself in a person, Jezebel first needs to get that person to hate authority and authority figures. My mom respected authority figures and she taught us to respect them, but Jezebel saw me as a candidate to not only operate as an Ahab; it saw my potential to be a Jezebel. For this reason, I became authoritative and controlling, but not towards my friends; I was controlling towards *some* men. Why *some* men? What I've since learned is that the Jezebel spirit recognizes other spirits more wicked than itself, so when I came in contact with men who had Ahab spirits or spirits weaker than the ones that were in me, I took charge of the relationship. Howbeit, the men who took charge of me were the ones who were craftier than I was. Sure, I wanted to be loved and, in most cases, my ultimate goal was to be loved, but love wasn't enough for me. I wanted to be respected; I needed to be respected. Anytime I felt disrespected, I would end the relationship. I think I was trying very hard to not be like my parents because I'd watched so many people take advantage of them and I did not want this to happen to me, so even as a young girl, I started experimenting with usurped authority. I respected my elders (for the most part), but if I came in contact with an older male who, for example, flirted with young women, I would not respect him. I would speak to him harshly and I would not treat him like an adult.

This is the web that Jezebel uses to capture and train young women and men to become Jezebels. It almost always starts at home. If a woman or man is born to a person who has the Jezebel spirit, in most cases, Jezebel will become a familiar spirit in that family and it will be passed down generation to generation. People often think that familiar spirits are nothing but divining spirits, but this is not always true. A familiar spirit is a family spirit, thus, the word *familiar*. It is a generational spirit that has established a stronghold on a particular bloodline. Howbeit, in order to activate the Jezebel in a person, that person needs to become bitter and starved of a particular need. In most cases, young Jezebels-in-training are starved of parental love, protection, or prayers. We are in a spiritual battle. Children have to be covered in prayer, otherwise, they are open for demonic attacks.

The enemy normally robs children of two-parent households so he can attack the child in the area where their present parent lacks understanding. For example, try as she may, a mother does not know how to teach her sons to be men. She can feed them, shelter them, pray for them and even teach them the Word of God, but she cannot relate to some of the challenges that they'll face as men. For this reason, Satan encourages fornication in this era because he thrives wherever there is a lack of knowledge. At the same time, the Jezebel spirit flourishes where disorder is present. Even though we don't like to admit this because single parenting is the norm these days, but it was never God's will for a child to be brought up without his or her father. The family unit represents a united front; it represents an impenetrable covering, so it goes without saying that Satan hates when two people come together in the name of the Lord. In other words, he hates families established together by Christ in Christ.

Matthew 18:20 (ESV): *For where two or three are gathered in my name, there am I among them.*

When families are created outside of Christ, Satan will utilize those families to create and establish bloodline curses before he attempts to rip them apart. Even when they are not in Christ, they still represent unity and Satan hates unity because he cannot function in it.

Genesis 11:6 (NLT): *"Look!" he said. "The people are united, and they all speak the same language. After this, nothing they set out to do will be impossible for them!*

Jezebels are recruited through bloodline curses (in many cases), but trained in pain. Of course, the Jezebel spirit can enter someone in their adult life and this usually happens when a person submits to another person who has the Jezebel spirit. In other words, they come under the Baal principality and essentially receive a demonic impartation. A good example of this is: sex, ungodly friendships, ungodly religions, churches with jezebellic leaders, ungodly friendships.

- When Jezebel recruits people through sex, it trains those people by using the folks they had sex with to hurt them ... *repeatedly.* This starts a vicious cycle of fornication, betrayal and abandonment. This cycle continues one relationship after the other.
- When Jezebel recruits people through friendships, it will train them by using the people they call friends to hurt them or lead them into false religions. What we need to be aware of is that not all ungodly friendships started off as ungodly. Some of them were established by God, but there came a time or a season when God wanted us to walk away, nevertheless, because of familiarity, we stuck around.
- When Jezebel recruits people through ungodly religions, it'll usually separate those people from their families. This starts a cycle of pain and rejection that filters over to their children and establishes generational curses.
- When Jezebel recruits people through jezebellic leaders, it is usually imparted through the laying on of hands or simply from them repeatedly being in a demonic environment. It then trains them through church hurt, demonic doctrines, confusion and finally, by causing them to despise church altogether. It causes them to think that all

churches and church folks are ungodly hypocrites with an agenda. In other words, Jezebel successfully projects her own image onto true believers. At the same time, many will not leave their churches, but will be trained to become Jezebels. They will learn to speak curses over anyone who does not agree with them; for example, when a person under a jezebellic leader comes to the leader and complains about another person, that leader will begin to speak evil over the person they are complaining about. She will then follow-up her witchcraft by saying things like, "This isn't witchcraft. We have the right, as believers, to stop foolishness like this from happening." What she's doing is training another Jezebel.

Gathering Ahabs

Who was Ahab in the Bible? He was the king of Israel. To understand how and why Jezebels gather Ahabs, we must first understand Ahab, the man.

Ahab was a king over God's people. This means that Ahab had authority. As a man, he was granted authority over his household and as a king, he was granted authority over God's people. Howbeit, Ahab was a fearful man who relinquished his authority in exchange for the ability to feel safe. By partnering with Phoenicia, he relinquished his authority and downplayed God's power. He was pretty much saying to the people of God that God could not and would not protect them. He was pretty much saying to the Phoenicians that he trusted in their gods more than he trusted in the God of Israel. Ahab behaved like many believers behave today. He still acknowledged God as “a” god, but he did not acknowledge Him as God all by Himself. For this reason, he allied himself with Jehoshaphat. When compelled to seek a prophecy from the Lord, Ahab sent for Micaiah, but because he hated truth, he hated Micaiah.

Ahab surrounded himself with false prophets and he did nothing as his wife slaughtered the true prophets of God. What's ironic is ... even though Ahab was so wicked, he still had some level of fear towards God. This is why he fasted after Elijah prophesied to him that God had already judged him (see 1 Kings 21:20-29).

Ahab was one of those people who thought that if he could silence the true prophets of God that he wouldn't be judged by God. He referred to Elijah as his enemy and he told Jehoshaphat that he hated Micaiah because he never prophesied anything good to him (1 Kings 22:8). There are many people like this today. They hate true prophets, even though they refer to themselves as Christians, show up at the church *building* every Sunday and read their Bibles faithfully. They have what is called a religious spirit, meaning, they have the appearance of power but deny the power thereof. They hate truth and are often heard justifying their sinful ways with, "God knows my heart" or "Let him who is without sin cast the first stone." They will ridicule, persecute and even attack the true prophets of God, all the while, trying to maintain their religious posts as Christians. These are the people who God spoke of when He said that many will come to Him and say, "Lord, Lord ... have we not prophesied in your name, cast out devils in your name and done many wonderful works in your name?" To this, God said that He will reply, "I never knew you: depart from me, you that work iniquity" (Matthew 7:22-23).

Again, Ahab was a man who had immeasurable authority that he was too afraid to walk in, but here's the thing: even if you deny the power of God, that does not stop it from existing. So what ends up happening is ... Jezebel comes and takes the authority from the person who's too afraid to walk in it. She then perverts that power and uses it against God's people. In other words, the enemy is able to illegally take authority over God's people through a person who legally has it. For example, a true godly man or woman can be the pastor of a church where they teach holiness and righteousness. However, that leader can become ensnared in Jezebel's trap and end up allowing Jezebel to teach at his or her church. Maybe the leader was drawn to the prophetic, but was too afraid to prophesy. Maybe the leader didn't test the spirits in the people they reached out to because they were too afraid to go up against them since other churches had welcomed them in. For whatever reason that leader allowed Jezebel to get behind the pulpit, the consequence is the same: God will address or punish that leader.

Revelation 2:20 (ESV): *But I have this against you, that you tolerate that woman Jezebel, who calls herself a prophetess and is teaching and seducing my servants to practice sexual immorality and to eat food sacrificed to idols.*

When Jezebel comes into leadership at someone's church, it is because Jezebel has successfully ahab'ed the leader of that church. This means that the leader will have to go through deliverance in order to restore the people of God.

Matthew 7:5 (ESV): *You hypocrite, first take the log out of your own eye, and then you will see clearly to take the speck out of your brother's eye.*

Jezebels gather Ahabs when they find:

- people who have legal authority, but are too

afraid to walk in it.

- people who lust for something that does not belong to them.
- people who have idols.

Jezebels gather Ahabs to access their authority and take control over the people, finances and things that the Ahabs have available to them. Remember, money equals power so Jezebels are attracted to people with decent jobs. This allows them to finance their agendas and draw subordinates to themselves. They gather these Ahabs by pretending to be the missing pieces in their lives, so wherever there is fear, Jezebel says, "Don't worry. I got this." Wherever there is a need, Jezebel says, "Don't worry. I can help."

Jezebels gather Ahabs in their neighborhoods, churches and in the workplace. For example, the local neighborhood Jezebel will often provide warm meals and parental support to any of the kids in that neighborhood who come from broken homes. The religious Jezebel will often provide advice and acceptance to a broken soul who enters the church suffering from rejection ... a person who wants love, but can't seem to find it or recognize it around them. To this, Jezebel says, "I want you" or "I love you." This is why so many people will defend a Jezebel who's been exposed. She was the first one to open her arms to them because the truth is that many people in the church today are too afraid to help people who don't look, behave, or think like themselves. Instead, they clutch their purses, hide their jewels, and intentionally sit as far away from those people as possible. After service, they will stop the broken souls and give them hugs but no love, and this allows Jezebel to intercept the broken souls and offer them what many in the church are not offering them: love when they feel unloved, acceptance when they feel rejected, security when they feel scared, and understanding when they feel misunderstood. In other words, we (the church) have failed to demonstrate the love of God and because of this, the Jezebel spirit is flourishing.

The workplace Jezebel normally catches people who either fear losing their jobs or are in some need of defense. You see, in every workplace, there are rules that even the managers must abide by, but many people are either ignorant of those rules or too afraid to enforce them. The way to enforce the rules when a manager is being unfair is simply by going to the manager's manager. Most folks fear doing this, so they opt to keep quiet. This is where Jezebel comes in and offers to defend them. Feeling appreciative and indebted to Jezebel, these people will follow her and relinquish their authority (the ability to enforce the workplace rules) to her in exchange for her protection.

Jezebels gather Ahabs through false religions, gangs and other ungodly associations. For example, many young men join gangs because they are tired of being bullied. They are fearful of the person or the people who've been bullying them, so the gang offers them a sense of protection. In truth, they are nothing but a group of Ahabs who've learned to trust in the power of numbers and weapons, rather than trusting in the power of God. *This is what Ahab, the man, did. He trusted in Phoenicia's numbers and weapons, but not God.* Their leaders are the Jezebels who lead them to their own destruction. Jezebels also gather Ahabs when people enter pride. For example, a man goes to college and gets a degree. He's the first and only person in his family who has gone to college in more than five generations. He then gets a really good job and acquires the respect of his family. However, because he's not guarded, the spirit of pride enters his life and begins to point out how *different* he is from his family. It pretty much tells him that he is superior to his family and that they will drag him down if allowed. His parents have always gone to church; they've always been religious, so he doesn't want to be like them. To differentiate himself from his family, he will likely enter a false religion or proclaim himself to be atheist or agnostic. This is because of pride. For this reason, he will become ahab'ed by the leaders of the very doctrine in which he serves. His new leaders will lead him further away from God so that they can establish themselves as god-like figures in his life. Understand this: the further he gets away from God, the more he will finance that religion and the more he will allow Jezebel to walk in his God-given authority.

Gathering Followers for Themselves

One of Jezebel's favorite webs to weave is a giant web that will allow them to capture as many people as possible. This includes religion, gangs and anyplace large groups of people come together. Howbeit, Jezebel doesn't necessarily have to be the face of power; it simply needs the ability to control the person who is in authority. For example, Jezebels don't always want to stand in the pulpit and lead the people; they simply want the ability to make a puppet out of the pastor who's leading the people. That's why many Jezebels will enter a church and immediately try to get close to the pastor. If the pastor won't receive them, they'll try to get close to someone who's close to the pastor. Their goal is to gather followers for themselves by becoming the pastor's mentor.

In the family unit, a Jezebel will try to coerce the family into following her. For example, Jezebels are very ambitious and will work tirelessly to get decent-paying jobs so that they can help out their families as much as possible. However, do not be deceived. This is not done out of love. Jezebel basically wants to buy their authority from them. This opens the family up for the spirit of poverty and allows Jezebel to be the hero anytime someone in the family is in need. Mara didn't go to college, nor did she have a good-paying job and this was one of the reasons she was so obsessed with controlling Roger. He had a really good-paying job, plus, in his culture, he was considered the prince of the family. This was no lavish position, however, what it meant was that he was his father's successor and the family had to call him whenever they had a problem that they themselves could not resolve. I didn't realize it then, but after he'd been named successor, he'd had to undergo a ritual so that he could receive the wisdom that the family would ultimately turn to him for. In other words, he had to receive a demonic impartation. So, Roger represented many things to Mara. He had the finances and the power to influence or control the family. However, he was a very passive man who honestly wanted to do right by his family. He was afraid to walk in his God-given authority, so Jezebel came in and walked in it for him.

While he was in college and building his career, Mara went and got herself a lot of credit cards. She used those credit cards to help any family member who needed help, but again, this was not done because of love; it was all centered around power. That's why she felt comfortable jumping on a plane and flying to another country with the intentions of putting her uncle's wife out of her own home. Her uncle asked for money and when she gave it to him, she felt that she had the power to control him in every way .... including his marriage. At the same time, she buried herself in credit card debt because she knew that she had full control over Roger. He'd gone to college in several countries to establish his trade and she knew that once he graduated, he would earn enough money to pay off her credit card debt.

In many families, Jezebel is the older family member who is said to be the very fabric of that family; she's the one who holds the family together, but not in a good way. Of course, there are some older men and women who are godly and they hold their families together in Christ, but Jezebels do just the opposite. They encourage and approve sin, all the while, ridiculing anyone who attempts to introduce any form of change to that family. Most Jezebels in the family unit are dominant and they utilize the power of the family to not only bind the family but to attack anyone who does not honor what they believe to be the familial code. However, Jezebels don't like to get their own hands dirty so, for example, if you were a family member and you were going to a God-fearing church where deliverance was taking place, the Jezebel leader in your family would first try to get you to stop going to that church. If this didn't work, she would call the family members who have the most influence in your life and tell them what *her* problem is with you. But first and foremost, before calling them, she will try to provoke you to anger; that way, you can say or do something that she and the rest of the family sees as disrespectful. This allows her to get the family members revved up (enraged) before she gets behind their "wills" and pretty much tells them what she wants from you. A good example would be if you were to hang up the phone in her face or tell her to mind her own business. After that, you'd likely be inundated with phone calls from angry family members demanding that you apologize to Jezebel and suggesting that you do whatsoever it is that she wants you to do. They'll say things like, "I don't always agree with Aunt May, but I personally don't see why you keep going to that church. Why don't you come to the church that the family goes to?" If this doesn't work, Jezebel will get the family to disassociate themselves from you.

Jezebels love to gather followers because this allows them to control as many people as possible. It also helps them to strengthen their control over each individual person under their stolen authority.

Destroying Godly Businesses

As a business owner, I have had my fair share of Jezebel encounters. My company works exclusively with Christian ministries and individuals looking to get seals and logos for their ministries or publish their Christian books. I've witnessed many demonic manifestations because I take something from people that equates to power and that is: *money*. Jezebels hate to separate from their money, but at the same time, they want to be able to promote themselves, their businesses, and their ministries. For this reason, they try to find ways to hold on to their money, all the while, getting whatever it is they feel can help them gather more followers.

I have come to recognize many demonic techniques that Jezebels use to coerce Christian businesses into giving them what they want. Some of these techniques include:

- **Flattery coupled with self-promotion:** I have received some of the most elaborate compliments when dealing with Jezebels. They will often go out of their way to make the business owner feel appreciated and needed, but beware; they will also try to get the business owner to think that he or she needs them. For example, one of the most common ploys I've witnessed is

Jezebels who say things like, "I can help your business explode. I know a lot of people and if this goes well between you and me, you're going to be a busy woman (or man)." This is an attempt to insert themselves into the business and get the owner to think that he or she needs them. My normal customers may compliment me, but they won't talk incessantly about themselves, nor do they attempt to promote the idea that they have the power in their hands to help my business explode. Instead, normal folks may compliment the business owner, ask a few questions and then, place their orders. They may even refer others. Anything more is normally a jezebellic attempt to gain control over the business by manipulating the business owner.

- **Divination:** Jezebels will often use divination and false prophecy to get the business owner in his or her emotions. Remember, Jezebel specializes in the realm of the flesh, so she has to get the business owner to step out of their professional role and get them to open themselves up to her emotionally. If the business owner falls for this, Jezebel will speak good things to them when she wants something from them or they are doing what she wants. However, when the business owner realizes that he or she can't give Jezebel the time, resources, and freebies that she wants and the business owner tries to regain authority over his or her own business, Jezebel will speak curses over the person and their business. She will also leave negative reviews and try to discourage others from doing business with that business owner.

- **Dominant control:** Some of my least favorite customers are the dominant Jezebels who attempt to gain authority over my business by angrily demanding what they want, how they want to do business and using their experience with another graphic designer or publisher as a justification for their ungodly attitudes. I've heard things like, "Hi, Tiffany. My name is Apostle, Dr. Mary Doe and I'm the founder of Mary Doe Ministries, Incorporated. My ministry has over two hundred members and growing, plus, I have churches in Africa and Asia. I am a no-nonsense type of person and I don't have time for games. I need a logo designed, but the last designer I had didn't do a good job, so I don't feel comfortable paying you upfront. So here's what's gonna happen, Tiffany. I'll submit the details for the logo to you and once you're done, just send me the sample. Once I approve it, I'll pay you. Like I said before, I've had someone to mess over me and I don't have time for games. Plus, I see on your website that Package A only comes with one revision. Look, I know you're in business to make money and I respect that, but there's no way I'm gonna pay you to revise something for me. I'll pay you once I'm satisfied with the work. I hope that's not a problem. Do you have a pen ready so I can tell you what I want?" Of course, this *never* works. I tell Jezebel how my company does business and that she has to fill out the form (I don't write down anything), pay the deposit (or full fee, depending on what she's ordering) and she's only allowed the amount of revisions allotted in the package that she chooses. In the beginning, the Jezebels would speak louder and restate how they want to do business, but nowadays, because I walk in the authority of Jesus Christ, they'll normally get off the phone with me and go elsewhere. I've had many young or new graphic designers to reach out to me because they were in the grips of some Jezebel who was controlling their businesses. I've actually met a few graphic designers who've closed their businesses because they grew tired of dealing with jezebellic customers.

- **Passive control:** A passive Jezebel will almost always come off as sweet, kind and understanding, but her demons will always manifest when she doesn't get her way. She will use flattery, self-pity, name-dropping or passive-aggressive tactics in an attempt to get what she wants. For example, she may say things like, "Did you finish with my logo? I noticed you were on Facebook earlier." This is her way of saying that she's watching the person or monitoring their behaviors. There have been a couple of cases where I've explained to people that business owners and designers do take breaks, however, they will receive their work in the time-frames promised. Another passive attempt I've witnessed is from people who say things like, "My former designer did it this way" or "My designer is out of town, but normally, he'll let me have as many revisions as I want." This is passive control. Now, this doesn't always mean that the person has a Jezebel, but it does mean that they are manifesting the traits of Jezebel. Anytime I've responded and said, for example, "Every designer is different and I don't operate by another designer's rules," the passive controller will respond and say, "Oh no, I wasn't implying that you work under their rules. I was just making a suggestion." In some cases, they will request a refund and then, they are shocked when I give it to them (if I haven't started working on their project or if I haven't sent out the work and can resale it). They are shocked and angry when I process the refund because the refund *isn't* what they wanted; it was a threat in the form of a refund request. They wanted me to work under their conditions and when I wouldn't do so, they thought that asking for a refund would scare me into working under their conditions. This doesn't work because God has blessed me with thousands of customers and the time I waste dealing with one controlling person is the time I could have worked with no less than four "delivered" souls. If a business owner gives in to this type of behavior, the Jezebel will cause that company to go out of business. That's because the Jezebel will force the business owner to put her needs over the needs of other customers and will use up most of the designer's time and resources. Another common ploy of a passive Jezebel is to tell the business owner or employee a sad story. A few years back, I kept finding myself on the phone with folks talking about how much they needed my services but couldn't afford them because of something they were going through. I had to stop this behavior to stay in business because they would waste a lot of my time. It got to the point where I was able to finish some folks' stories before they finished them.

- **Rebelling against the company's posted rules:** Jezebels passionately hate rules so much that they'll even challenge the smallest of them. For example, a store employee can tell Jezebel to do something as simple as stand in line and Jezebel will threaten that employee's job. I've seen this happen many times, having worked in retail. Jezebels think that the rules don't apply to them and if you try to make them abide by the rules, they'll usually explode with anger. However, to get past the rules, Jezebels will either try to incite fear in the business owner or manager or she'll try to use flattery. Fear is her favorite weapon because it opposes faith. Her web of control is strengthened by the authority that she's managed to undermine from the highest authority in that particular business. In other words, she usurps the authority of the authority figure and begins to walk in it. She'll even tell employees that she can make one phone call and cost them their jobs.
- **Rebelling against the company's pricing:** One common feat you'll witness Jezebel perform is to get some companies to give her services and products at discounted prices. The way she does this is by asking to speak with the highest au-

thority available in that business. She may even point out flaws in the product or service in her attempt to get a discount. Now, don't get me wrong. I think we've all found the last of something in a store and saw that it was chipped or broken and we've brought it to the cashier's attention to get a discount. However, with Jezebel, this is not a one-time event; it's commonplace. In local businesses, Jezebels are oftentimes recognized by the managers and the employees the minute they walk in through the door. They have been known to break, chip or deface items in an attempt to get discounts. Jezebels will also try to talk a service-provider down on their prices; for example, they may tell the provider how much another company charges. They are very crafty spirits who don't like to separate from their money or feel as if they are not in control. They love having the ability to boast to others about what they've managed to accomplish through dominance or manipulation. It's not uncommon to hear Jezebel say, for example, "I always get a discount when I go to that store. All you have to do is ask for the manager with the red hair. I think her name is Donna. When she comes to the front, just act like you're mad and she'll give you a discount." What Jezebel has done is found an Ahab in authority who she can control and she will tell others how to control that Ahab.

- **Attempting to take as much of the businesses' time and resources as possible:** Jezebels are known to be time-wasting and time-consuming spirits that, if allowed, will turn a company into a one-man-show where they're the only customers getting serviced. They are the reasons that many companies have had to repeatedly change their rules or have had to close their doors. If there are no rules, Jezebels will never be satisfied with a product or a service; they will always request changes and they'll want to take up as much time speaking with the authority figure as possible. Again, this is to create a soul tie with the person in authority. They will talk to you about their kids, their grand kids, their goldfish, their health problems and anything they can think of while your customers stand in line behind them waiting for their turns. If one or more of the customers in line is to get frustrated and walk out, Jezebels have been known to chuckle. I've had to remind a few customers that I do have other customers who are trying to call in on the line that they are holding up. I've had customers who thought I was going to stay on the phone with them while I worked on their projects. Jezebels

> will use up as much time and resources as they are allowed to use. If the authority figure in that business does not utilize his or her own authority and enforce the rules, the business will become a lawless establishment centered around Jezebel and her rules. It won't be long for such a company to close its doors indefinitely.

Statistics state that 80 percent of businesses close within the first year and what I've learned is that most Christian businesses close because of Jezebel. For example, another fellow web designer stated that she was closing her web design business. When I asked her why, she said it was because many of her customers wanted a lot of changes and could never really seem to be satisfied. She said that she wasn't really making any money because of those types of customers. Of course, I told her to place up some new rules. For example, with my company, my customers have to send in *everything* they want on their websites *before* I start the design. This is to prevent some of my customers from doing what I've seen many of them do in the past and that is ... get excited after seeing the website for the first time, and then, decide to send me a week's worth of work after the site is finished. This cycle would never stop if the designer does not take control of the situation. This leads to the site having to be reworked and sometimes, redesigned. I tell them that anything sent after I start the design is a new order and it's followed by a new order fee. The new order fee ensures that I am compensated for the extra time should the customer request extra work. This has made my web company run a lot smoother than it used to because people don't want to pay out more money than they have to, so they send me *everything* they want on the site *before* I start the design. At the same time, since Jezebels don't like to part with their money (unless they are purchasing the ability to control someone), they won't normally place extensive orders with me. I've learned that whenever I have a problem, I need to establish a solution to keep that problem from becoming fatal to my business and allowing Jezebel to come in and waste my time or resources. I've learned that in order to keep Jezebel from spinning me into her web, I have to establish and enforce rules, even if that means I have to offend some people and even ban some people. This has worked out well because I have a friendly, professional and godly relationship with 98-99 percent of my customers. With them, I don't have to state the rules or enforce them. They've already read about them and agreed to them because they don't want power and control; they want the services that I'm offering. Jezebels want power *and* service. When I do get that one customer who begins to manifest the Jezebel spirit, I send them to the page where the rules are posted. Additionally, I enforce those rules and charge them extra fees for extra time. This keeps Jezebel away from my business and allows my business to flourish. It also allows me to keep my peace and to keep my customers happy.

Destroying Families

Every group who is united is considered a body and every individual person in that group is referred to as a member. For example, we are all members of the body of Christ. We are also members of our collective families. We all bring something to the groups that we are a part of.

Additionally, every group has a head. The head represents the authority figure; the one who determines the direction of that group. In churches, the pastor is the head. He or she determines the direction of that church. In marriage, the husband is the head. He is the one who determines the direction of that family. God must be the head of the pastor, otherwise, He won't be the head of that church; the pastor will. And without God, the church would be led by an ungodly pastor. God must be the head of the husband, otherwise, He won't be the head of that family; the person who takes control would be the head, whether it's the wife, the husband or the children. This would render the marriage an ungodly union. Now, it goes without saying that each individual in a church or a family *can* and *should* have their own personal relationship with God and God *can* and *should* be the head of that person. Nevertheless, if the person is unequally yoked with a ministry or spouse, that person will find himself or herself enduring a lot of warfare. The reason for this is ... the people who are not serving God will be ungodly vessels whom the enemy will use to wreak havoc on anyone and everyone who serves God. God gives us all free will and if a ministry head or a family member *chooses* to not follow or submit to Him, we weren't supposed to be linked up to that ministry or that person in the first place. This means that somewhere, somehow, we disobeyed God and unequally yoked ourselves with unbelievers.

2 Corinthians 6:14-18 (ESV): *Do not be unequally yoked with unbelievers. For what partnership has righteousness with lawlessness? Or what fellowship has light with darkness? What accord has Christ with Belial? Or what portion does a believer share with an unbeliever? What agreement has the temple of God with idols? For we are the temple of the living God; as God said, "I will make my dwelling among them and walk among them, and I will be their God, and they shall be my people. Therefore go out from their midst, and be separate from them, says the Lord, and touch no unclean thing; then I will welcome you, and I will be a father to you, and you shall be sons and daughters to me, says the Lord Almighty."*

But what if the Jezebel is in our extended families; for example, what if you're a single, adult woman whose family is full of Jezebels? Who then is the head of that family? Please understand this. In the collective, extended family unit, there is no established head. This means that each individual adult is the head of his or her own home, but in the extended family unit, there are oftentimes people who rise up and operate as the overall authority figures. Therefore, if Jezebel is the authority over that family or if Jezebel is tolerated in that family, it is better for you to not be a member of it; meaning, you have to separate yourself from your natural family to follow your supernatural family. The blood of Jesus Christ separated you from the bloodline curses in your natural family. This isn't a popular truth, however, it is necessary for us to maintain Christ as the head of our lives and that we don't make ourselves a part of anything that Jezebel is functioning in or leading.

Matthew 10:34-39 (ESV): *Do not think that I have come to bring peace to the earth. I have not come to bring peace, but a sword. For I have come to set a man against his father, and a daughter against her mother, and a daughter-in-law against her mother-in-law. And a person's enemies will be those of his own household. Whoever loves father or mother more than me is not worthy of me, and whoever loves son or daughter more than me is not worthy of me. And whoever does not take his cross* *and follow me is not worthy of me. Whoever finds his life will lose it, and whoever loses his life for my sake will find it.*

2 Corinthians 6:17 (ESV): *Therefore go out from their midst, and be separate from them, says the Lord, and touch no unclean thing; then I will welcome you, and I will be a father to you, and you shall be sons and daughters to me, says the Lord Almighty.*

The Jezebel spirit destroys the family unit by polluting the bloodline and establishing ungodly traditions in a family. For example, in some cultures and households, children are taught that their siblings and parents are the most important people in their lives, including when they get married. They are taught to put their parents and their siblings above their spouses and children. This is a Jezebel-instituted tradition designed to keep the order of God out of those families, thus, allowing Satan to be the head of those families. Basically, what the Jezebel spirit does is causes each individual in that family to reverence tradition over the Word of God. Jezebel thrives in disorder and anytime you come across disorder, Jezebel is responsible for it.

Genesis 2:24 (ESV): *Therefore a man shall leave his father and his mother and hold fast to his wife, and they shall become one flesh.*

1 Corinthians 15:33 (ESV): *Do not be deceived: "Bad*

company ruins good morals."

Extended family units can be good when the people in them are servants of God and Jezebel is not tolerated. In a godly family, those who wear the crown of wisdom (the elderly) will often function as the heads. By being a godly unit, each person essentially becomes what is best described as a counselor and a sharpening tool designed to help each member who needs sharpening.
Proverbs 16:31 (ESV): *Gray hair is a crown of glory; it is gained in a righteous life.*
Job 12:12 (ESV): *Wisdom is with the aged, and understanding in length of days.*
Proverbs 27:17 (ESV): *Iron sharpens iron, and one man sharpens another.*

One of the hardest things to tell someone is that he or she needs to separate himself or herself from their natural family. I've witnessed countless people attempt to tolerate Jezebel in the name of love, and sadly enough, they keep going through one attack after the other until they finally come to accept that God is calling them from amongst the familiarity of their families. This can be very disheartening as we all want to have that strong family unit that we can laugh with, cry with, and pray with; but in truth, this is not the reality for the majority of us ... especially prophets. What I've learned is that many, if not most, true prophets are born into families where the Jezebel spirit thrives and is tolerated. I believe God allows this so that the prophet can get the training he or she needs to discern Jezebel, confront Jezebel, and eventually push her off her wall. But first, prophets need to be able to separate themselves from their natural families and renounce the traditions and bloodline curses that came in through those families. This is the hardest part of the prophetic mantle; this is where most prophets fail because they refuse to let go of the people God has told them to walk away from. So, they end up becoming religious, legalistic eunuchs in their attempts to find some medium where they can have God, all the while, tolerating Jezebel. This bridge simply does *not* exist and, for this reason, such prophets end up enduring a lot of unnecessary warfare, confusion, and depression. Depression is oftentimes the presence of purpose coupled with the absence of action. It's hopelessness and anxiety birthed through idleness and idolatry.

I've witnessed some people successfully walk away from their families and surrender their lives to God. What's amazing is God has used many of those folks to lead even the most stubborn Jezebels in their families to Christ. God first had to separate them, change them and then, make them into living demonstrations of His power. In some cases, when this happened, the estranged family watched from afar as God's miraculous power made itself evident in their family members' lives. Please note that there are the ones who won't be saved because, simply put, they don't want to be delivered. We must remember that God has created us all and He witnesses countless people rejecting Him and refusing deliverance every Planck of a day. I've witnessed some prophets who refused to walk away from their families. Instead, to justify sticking around, they will become religious and start saying things like, "Even Jesus sat with sinners" or "I think God wants to use me to lead my family to Christ." Unfortunately, in every case where I've witnessed this, the believers kept enduring one attack after the other until they returned to the Egyptian wildernesses that they were familiar with. In other words, they returned to Jezebel and all of the familiar spirits in their families. *I suspect that this is how Jezebel managed to kill so many of God's prophets when she reigned as queen over Israel.* I've come to learn that the lesson is almost always getting us (the believers) to *actually* believe what the Word of God says. It is to get us to understand that the Word of God *does* apply to us, even when it hurts! Many believers have found themselves in the wilderness emotionally, financially and spiritually simply because they attempted to lead people to God who saw no reason to follow Him. Surprisingly enough, this is an attempt to usurp power, meaning, if God won't *force* them to serve Him, who are we to *force* folks to serve Him? For this reason, they were being led astray by their families and Satan helped them to justify tolerating Jezebel by telling them that they were to accept Jezebel's abuse and just be a light. The problem is ... when people love what's dwelling in the darkness of their hearts, they will cut off (strike against) the lights! So the misguided believers learn to sit at the dinner table, turn their lights off, behave as carnally as they're expected to behave and accept Jezebel's abuse. In exchange, they expect to gain the approval of the folks who have rejected the very God they claim to serve! In other words, Satan taught them to become religious, unapologetic Ahabs and eunuchs who essentially started hating the truth and anyone who spoke it.

Romans 1:21-32 (ESV): *For although they knew God, they did not honor him as God or give thanks to him, but they became futile in their thinking, and their foolish hearts were darkened. Claiming to be wise, they became fools, and exchanged the glory of the immortal God for images resembling mortal man and birds and animals and creeping things.*

Therefore God gave them up in the lusts of their hearts to impurity, to the dishonoring of their bodies among themselves, because they exchanged the truth about God for a lie and worshiped and served the creature rather than

the Creator, who is blessed forever! Amen.
For this reason God gave them up to dishonorable passions. For their women exchanged natural relations for those that are contrary to nature; and the men likewise gave up natural relations with women and were consumed with passion for one another, men committing shameless acts with men and receiving in themselves the due penalty for their error.
And since they did not see fit to acknowledge God, God gave them up to a debased mind to do what ought not to be done. They were filled with all manner of unrighteousness, evil, covetousness, malice. They are full of envy, murder, strife, deceit, maliciousness. They are gossips, slanderers, haters of God, insolent, haughty, boastful, inventors of evil, disobedient to parents, foolish, faithless, heartless, ruthless. Though they know God's righteous decree that those who practice such things deserve to die, they not only do them but give approval to those who practice them.

I've witnessed men and women allow the Jezebels in their families to destroy their marriages and traumatize their children. Sure, we are all taught by our families, but I've come to understand that we can't blame what we're taught for our choices; it's what we've come to believe that has the greatest power.

Destroying Marriages

Anytime I've witnessed a Jezebel-Ahab marriage, one of the things I've noticed is the Ahab in that marriage tends to idolize and worship the Jezebel who's stolen his or her authority. Such couples are hard to counsel because the Jezebel spirit in one partner is only there because it's married to the Ahab spirit in the other partner. This is what is normally called a spirit husband or a spirit wife. Such a marriage has to be torn down before it can be re-established on a godly foundation. The Ahab in that marriage has to renounce the spirit of idolatry, the spirit of Ahab and whatever other spirits they may have. They have to repent of their idolatry and return to God wholeheartedly. This is difficult for the ahab'ed person because it puts their marriage in immediate danger. To them, it appears that they are abandoning their marriages, even though they aren't being physically separated from their spouses. In truth, they are abandoning the spiritual spouse that is in operation and the Jezebel in that marriage will manifest and begin to threaten them with divorce. Because they are spiritually blind and obsessed with Jezebel, they will fear her threats and return to their Jezebel-assigned posts (in most cases). Sadly enough, because the foundation of those marriages is not love, it is very hard to get both parties to divorce the spirits in that marriage so they can truly come together in Christ Jesus.

Additionally, one of the most common reasons for divorce today, outside of adultery, is having a Jezebellic mother-in-law who is hell-bent on controlling her son's wife or destroying his marriage altogether. This doesn't just happen with mother-in-laws (obviously), but it is most common with them. Jezebel sees her son (for example) as her property and she sees her daughter-in-law as both a trespasser *and* a pacifier for her son. The wife is a trespasser because what's in the mother (Jezebel) is married to what's in the son (Ahab). The wife is a pacifier because the mother knows that she cannot have a romantic relationship with her son. At the same time, she may not be entertaining the idea of having a romantic relationship with her son, but that does not stop her from reacting like a jealous wife when her son is romantically involved with someone else. Having a wife helps to keep him settled, so the mother will see the benefit of the wife, all the while, wishing she could find a way to get him (her son) to be content as a single man. A mother-in-law who's like this will be confused regarding her emotions for her son, so to justify behaving in such an inordinate fashion, she will look for flaws in her daughter-in-law. She will then point out those flaws and say, "This is why I don't like her." Nevertheless, if she manages to destroy her son's marriage and he is to marry another woman, the mother would still find a reason to not like the new bride. Again, that's because the Jezebel in her is married to the Ahab in her son and she doesn't know how to express her true feelings, giving that they are usual, psychotic, and demonic. In most cases like this, the mother will try to find a woman for her son that she can easily control which, of course, is a woman who has the Ahab spirit. This won't stop her from feeling jealous anytime she sees her son with his wife, but it does allow her to push his wife aside without conflict and to take everything from her (especially children) that she feels entitled to.

Destroying Churches and Prophets

Again, the church represents a unit and it consists of the head and the members. Every individual member is a church and each individual member will either worship God in Spirit and in Truth, or they will worship some other deity. All too often, believers find themselves worshiping the image of God, but not the reality of Him. This means that many believers today are worshiping what they believe to be God, but is not actually Him. *How so?* Because so many people have come to love their sins and so many leaders have allowed sin to possess the land, the church (for the most part) has become desensitized to and tolerable of sin.

You can be in Sunday service at your local church assembly praising God, all the while, standing next to people who are not praising the true and living God. They are praising a god they've accepted in their hearts ... one who accepts their fornications, hatred, strife, envy, and deceptive ways. In their hearts, they believe that they don't have to change for God; instead, He has to change His Word for them. They are idolaters and lovers of filthy lucre (money) who've come to believe that they can be as sinful as they want to be and God has no choice but to accept them and their sins. They have become religious Rachels, whereas, they are standing amongst believers, all the while, hiding their idols in their hearts. This is indeed the Jezebel spirit in operation. It hates true worship, but loves religion, idolatry, and deception.

Genesis 31:33-35 (ESV): *So Laban went into Jacob's tent and into Leah's tent and into the tent of the two female servants, but he did not find them. And he went out of Leah's tent and entered Rachel's. Now Rachel had taken the household gods and put them in the camel's saddle and sat on them. Laban felt all about the tent, but did not find them. And she said to her father, "Let not my lord be angry that I cannot rise before you, for the way of women is upon me." So he searched but did not find the household gods.*

Many pastors have come under fire because they've taken a stand against something that God speaks against (fornication, homosexuality, etc.). Ironically enough, it was one of the church's members who videotaped their pastors' sermons and then, attempted to "expose" them. This is the way of the Jezebel spirit. It hates truth and deliverance, so it will go into a church and sit amongst true believers, waiting on an opportunity to "expose" the pastor. We live in the age of technology, where many members are now sitting in churches, videotaping the sermons, and waiting for "their" opportunities to go viral at the expense of souls. They don't mind destroying an entire church for the opportunity to gather followers for themselves. Again, this is the way of the Jezebel spirit. Jezebel is self-centered, prideful, and never accepts responsibility for her own actions.

Jezebel's ultimate goal is to destroy the unity and sanctity of the church family and to extinguish all of God's true prophets. Its goal is promote the worship of Baal and establish its own government in place of God's government. It does this by going against the Word of God in every way imaginable. It is the spirit behind every form of disorder you see in the church today, including the acceptance of pagan holidays (ex: Halloween), pagan gods (ex: Eostre) and pagan practices (ex: yoga). By getting the world and the church to agree on its agenda, it can successfully cause an uproar against the true prophets of God and anyone who dares speak the uncompromising truth. It has successfully shut the mouths of so many believers using its favorite spirit of fear (Ahab). It has divided the church and reduced many of God's people to becoming blind followers of religions and religious leaders, instead of God. It funds its agenda using the time and resources of confused believers who are too lazy to have an intimate relationship with God, therefore, they have to accept whatever their leaders tell them as truth. Like the signals that pass through our television sets, the Jezebel spirit has managed to find ways to get the world and the church's eyes fixated on individual people who Jezebel channels her lies, agendas, and witchcraft through. Today's church is in trouble because many believers are following the world's "celebrated ones" or celebrities and have come into agreement with them. Those same believers are the ones who are responsible for "exposing" pastors and criticizing anyone who dares to speak the uncompromising Word of God. This is why God told us to separate ourselves from the world, because by doing so, we reject the world's influence and we won't become desensitized to sin. Half of the folks who agree with new world practices, homosexuality, fornication and anything the world has accepted are in the church masquerading themselves as Christians. How is this a masquerade? Because it is impossible to serve two gods! However, the title "Christian" is just that: a title that helps to identify the beliefs a person *allegedly* has or identifies with. Howbeit, being Christian and Christ-like are not one and the same.

Matthew 6:22-24 (ESV): *The eye is the lamp of the body. So, if your eye is healthy, your whole body will be full of light, but if your eye is bad, your whole body will be full of darkness. If then the light in you is darkness, how great is the darkness!*

No one can serve two masters, for either he will hate the one and love the other, or he will be devoted to the one and despise the other. You cannot serve God and money.

Jezebel hates the prophets of God; we know this. Satan always tries to copy whatever God does, so he has sent out false prophets to mislead the world and Jezebel is the queen of the false prophets. There are two types of false prophets. The first one is a person who uses familiar spirits to prophesy. This means that such a person is using divinity and is bound by the python spirit. The second false prophet is a person who intentionally tells lies and disguises their lies as prophecies. They normally do this for financial gain or popularity and they normally give general information to whomever it is they claim to be prophesying to. For example, a false prophet may say something like, "I see you've been hurt, but God says He's going to restore you" or "There's been a lot of contention in your family." You see, both of these messages apply to just about everyone! Now, this doesn't mean that if a prophet gives you a word of knowledge or a prophecy (the two are not the same) that sounds generic that he or she is a false prophet. What I am saying is that a lot of false prophets who *intentionally* tell lies give out generic information!

One of the things that Jezebel is doing with today's church is filling its pulpits with demonically led leaders who, unbeknownst to them, are being raised up to fall. Jezebel's goal is to embarrass the church by disguising false prophets as true men and women of God, overwhelming those people with lusts and then, exposing them for the world to see! The goal here is to discredit the church altogether. It's to make people say, "This is why I don't go to church." It is to keep people away from corporate unity because Jezebel hates unity. She thrives where there is division, but unity renders her weak and exposes her altogether. This is why Jezebels sow discord amongst members and amongst the church as a whole. She encourages religious divides to keep the church as divided as possible so she can accomplish her ungodly agenda. What is that agenda again? It is to establish Baal worship wherever it hasn't been established and to rid the world of God's people and His prophets. Any remaining people must renounce God and turn to Baal; this is the agenda of the Jezebel spirit.

Jezebel's Unraveling

Jezebel's goal is unmistakable. She wants to destroy the church; she wants to destroy the family unit, and she wants to destroy God's people ... especially His prophets. But here's a truth that is rarely visited: Jezebel cannot operate outside of the church's authority. What does this mean? It means that if we'd allowed that foreign spirit to stay amongst the pagans and we didn't invite it into our churches, our homes and our pulpits, it would not be the powerful principality it is today. Remember this: when Ahab, the man, met Jezebel, the woman, he was the king of God's people, whereas, Jezebel was a pagan princess. She should never have been given a title of authority over God's people. The same is true for the many Jezebels that are thriving in today's churches, homes, Christian businesses and Christian connections. The truth of the matter is ... most of us have tolerated Jezebel or are tolerating Jezebel. We are too afraid to open our mouths and proclaim what the Word of God says because we don't want to deal with the secular or the religious backlash that follows. This means that the average Christian does not want to pick up their crosses and follow Jesus. The cross represents persecution, rejection, suffering and above all, the cross represents unyielding love. This means that we have to find a love that's greater than ourselves and endure the stripes that we'll receive as we preach and teach the *uncompromising* Word of God. We do this because we love God and we want to lead as many people to salvation as possible. Howbeit, many in the church are caught up in Jezebel's web of deception, whereas, they've settled for the American dream, even at the risk of being faced with an everlasting nightmare called fire and brimstone. Many of us have established comfort zones in our bondage and we have allowed the witch, Jezebel, to scare us into submission. That's why God has hidden many of His true prophets, to be revealed in an instant to do the work that many in the church are too afraid (or too compromised) to do. If He revealed the locations of all of His true prophets, Jezebel would systematically seek to destroy them and she'd use "church folks" to attack and "expose" any error found in them. For this reason, God has hidden many of the prophets who are fully submitted to Him and these men and women of God will not be afraid of corporate persecution, ridicule, or death! He is raising up the Jehu generation ... a group of men and women who will not be afraid to confront Jezebel and destroy Ahab's lineage. Please understand that judgment has already been pronounced on the household of Ahab and the people who submit to the Jezebel-Ahab order will fall under that same judgment.

1 Kings 19:18 (ESV): *"Yet I will leave seven thousand in Israel, all the knees that have not bowed to Baal, and ev-*

ery mouth that has not kissed him."

Jezebel's web will be unraveled one deceived soul at a time and even though her plans look like they're working, they are not. Anytime we see a great falling away of righteousness, God is only setting the stage for Him to perform the miraculous and show, once again, that He and only He is the true and living God!

1 Kings 18:17-40 (ESV): *When Ahab saw Elijah, Ahab said to him, "Is it you, you troubler of Israel?" And he answered, "I have not troubled Israel, but you have, and your father's house, because you have abandoned the commandments of the Lord and followed the Baals. Now therefore send and gather all Israel to me at Mount Carmel, and the 450 prophets of Baal and the 400 prophets of Asherah, who eat at Jezebel's table."*

So Ahab sent to all the people of Israel and gathered the prophets together at Mount Carmel. And Elijah came near to all the people and said, "How long will you go limping between two different opinions? If the Lord is God, follow him; but if Baal, then follow him." And the people did not answer him a word. Then Elijah said to the people, "I, even I only, am left a prophet of the Lord, but Baal's prophets are 450 men. Let two bulls be given to us, and let them choose one bull for themselves and cut it in pieces and lay it on the wood, but put no fire to it. And I will prepare the other bull and lay it on the wood and put no fire to it. And you call upon the name of your god, and I will call upon the name of the Lord, and the God who answers by fire, he is God." And all the people answered, "It is well spoken." Then Elijah said to the prophets of Baal, "Choose for yourselves one bull and prepare it first, for you are many, and call upon the name of your god, but put no fire to it." And they took the bull that was given them, and they prepared it and called upon the name of Baal from morning until noon, saying, "O Baal, answer us!" But there was no voice, and no one answered. And they limped around the altar that they had made. And at noon Elijah mocked them, saying, "Cry aloud, for he is a god. Either he is musing, or he is relieving himself, or he is on a journey, or perhaps he is asleep and must be awakened." And they cried aloud and cut themselves after their custom with swords and lances, until the blood gushed out upon them. And as midday passed, they raved on until the time of the offering of the oblation, but there was no voice. No one answered; no one paid attention.

Then Elijah said to all the people, "Come near to me." And all the people came near to him. And he repaired the altar of the Lord that had been thrown down. Elijah took twelve stones, according to the number of the tribes of the sons of Jacob, to whom the word of the Lord came, saying, "Israel shall be your name," and with the stones he built an altar in the name of the Lord. And he made a trench about the altar, as great as would contain two seahs of seed. And he put the wood in order and cut the bull in pieces and laid it on the wood. And he said, "Fill four jars with water and pour it on the burnt offering and on the wood." And he said, "Do it a second time." And they did it a second time. And he said, "Do it a third time." And they did it a third time. And the water ran around the altar and filled the trench also with water.

And at the time of the offering of the oblation, Elijah the prophet came near and said, "O Lord, God of Abraham, Isaac, and Israel, let it be known this day that you are God in Israel, and that I am your servant, and that I have done all these things at your word. Answer me, O Lord, answer me, that this people may know that you, O Lord, are God, and that you have turned their hearts back." Then the fire of the Lord fell and consumed the burnt offering and the wood and the stones and the dust, and licked up the water that was in the trench. And when all the people saw it, they fell on their faces and said, "The Lord, he is God; the Lord, he is God." And Elijah said to them, "Seize the prophets of Baal; let not one of them escape." And they seized them. And Elijah brought them down to the brook Kishon and slaughtered them there.

CHAPTER 4

Understanding Your Armor

Sometimes, we find ourselves in an ongoing battle with the Jezebel spirit simply because we are:

1. Not wearing the whole armor of God.
2. We're trying to fight while wearing the wrong armor.
3. We're bound by our brethren's opinions of us.
4. We have not severed the head of the serpent.
5. We are submitted to the wrong leaders.
6. We keep getting promoted by the devil who's trying to kill us.
7. We keep romantically engaging ourselves with people under Jezebel's control.
8. We keep tolerating Jezebel.
9. We are not utilizing our opportunities to kill Jezebel.

Either way, anytime we are not properly covered, we open ourselves for demonic attack.

Not Wearing the Whole Armor of God

Ephesians 6:10-20 (ESV): *Finally, be strong in the Lord* *and in the strength of his might. Put on the whole armor of God, that you may be able to stand against the schemes of the devil. For we do not wrestle against flesh and blood, but against the rulers, against the authorities, against the cosmic powers over this present darkness, against the spiritual forces of evil in the heavenly places. Therefore take up the whole armor of God, that you may be able to withstand in the evil day, and having done all, to stand firm. Stand therefore, having fastened on the belt of truth, and having put on the breastplate of righteousness, and, as shoes for your feet, having put on the readiness given by the gospel of peace. In all circumstances take up the shield of faith, with which you can extinguish all the flaming darts of the evil one; and take the helmet of salvation, and the sword of the Spirit, which is the word of God, praying at all times in the Spirit, with all prayer and supplication. To that end, keep alert with all perseverance, making supplication for all the saints, and also for me, that words may be given to me in opening my mouth boldly to proclaim the mystery of the gospel, for which I am an ambassador in chains, that I may declare it boldly, as I ought to speak.*

There are six parts to the armor of God and they are:

- **The belt of truth**
- **The breastplate of righteousness**
- **The shield of faith**

- **The helmet of salvation**
- **Feet prepared with the gospel of peace**
- **The sword of the Spirit**

Each part to the armor plays an important role in our protection and deliverance. One of the things people commonly ask while under attack is, "Why didn't God protect me?" or "Why didn't God prevent this from happening?" The truth is ... God gave us the ability to protect ourselves. We have to clothe ourselves in the full armor of God, otherwise, we are open for attack. Think of it this way. Some police departments issue bulletproof vests to their officers. Whether the officers wear the vest is completely up to each individual officer. If Officer John Doe, for example, does not wear the vest and he's shot in the abdomen, he cannot say the police department did not protect him. They gave him the tools to protect himself, however, he chose not to utilize those tools.

The belt of truth is the Word of God. We are to unashamedly share the gospel of Jesus Christ without altering or diluting it in *any* way. To share the truth, we must know the truth and that's why the Word tells us to study and show ourselves approved (2 Timothy 2:15). The truth also protects us from the lies and the deception of the enemy; after all, the Bible tells us that in the last days, many false prophets will arise and lead others astray (Matthew 24:11). The Word also says that false christs and false prophets will display signs, miracles and wonders, and *if* it were possible, they'd deceive the very elect of God (Matthew 24:24). For this reason, we need the belt of truth. Lastly, we need the belt of truth because if we preach any other gospel than the gospel of Jesus Christ, we will bring a curse upon ourselves (Galatians 1:8-9).

The breastplate of righteousness is our fruit of faith. The Bible tells us that Abram (later renamed Abraham) believed God and it was accounted to him as righteousness (Genesis 15:6). What does this mean? Abram didn't just hear a word; he believed the Word he heard. This was the fruit of his faith.

Righteousness is established through faith; it is marked by us not only believing in God but also by us believing God. It is characterized by our words and demonstrated through our choices. This is our fruit. God told Abram that his offspring would be as numerous as the stars. Abram was old and he was at a stage and an age where normally, he shouldn't have been able to have children ... especially with his wife, Sarai (later renamed Sarah). Nevertheless, the Bible tells us that Abram believed God and God accounted this to him as righteousness.

The enemy is always trying to make us doubt God; that way, we won't be guarded by the breastplate of righteousness. Nevertheless, we must hold the truth in our hearts and refuse to let go of it, regardless of what we see manifesting before our eyes.

The shield of faith is knowing the Word and believing the Word. It is trusting God, even though you can't see Him. It is believing that He has and will do everything He said He will do. It is believing that Jesus Christ is the Son of God, and we can't just say this with our mouths; the Word tells us that we must also believe this in our hearts (Romans 10:9). Many people confess what they do not believe and that's why God said in Matthew 15:8 (ESV), "This people honors me with their lips, but their heart is far from me." This is to teach us that not everyone who declares that Jesus Christ is Lord actually believes that He is Lord. Many people have doubt in their hearts, but they are religious parakeets, saying what they've heard others say.

We can't just display the shield of faith; we must possess faith in order to have a shield to protect ourselves against the enemy's fiery darts. Those darts include accusations, persecution, demonic attacks, witchcraft and so on. Without the shield of faith, we become warriors without protection. We must know the Word to have faith in the Word. Remember, faith comes by hearing and hearing by the Word of God (Romans 10:17).

The helmet of salvation comes through faith. We must believe that Jesus Christ is the Son of God; He died for our sins, rose on the third day and is now seated at the right hand of God making intercession for us (Romans 10:9). Faith doesn't end there. We must also believe and declare that every Word that proceeded from the mouth of God is true (Matthew 4:4). This is our helmet; it protects our head, or better yet, our authority.

A man's head is his control center; it is the part that houses his thoughts and beliefs. Biblically speaking, it is also the part that houses his heart. In the natural, we refer to the central red organ that distributes blood to our entire body as our hearts. But when the Bible speaks of a man's heart, it is speaking of the place where his beliefs are stored. It is where we store up the Word and it is the very source that we pour out from. To wear the helmet of salvation, a man's heart must be guarded (Proverbs 4:23), otherwise, the enemy will access his belief system and begin to contaminate him. That's how so many false religions spring up. There are many people who are open to hearing religions and religious leaders teach a different gospel other than the gospel of Jesus Christ. That's why in these days, you will see people who preach the gospel suddenly renounce the Lord and start following a different deity. They weren't wearing the helmet of salvation. They preached a gospel that they themselves were unsure of and because of this, the enemy sent people to pervert, corrupt and mislead them.

Feet prepared with the gospel of peace is to have a readiness to share the Word of God with anyone who is willing to hear it. It is to teach in love and humility; it is to walk in forgiveness and a readiness to forgive when offended. It is to maintain your peace and promote peace wherever you go. Jesus said in Matthew 5:9 (ESV), "Blessed are the peacemakers, for they shall be called sons of God."

The sword of the Spirit is the Word of God. It is a weapon used for offense and defense. It is the power of the Holy Spirit. Satan is often described as a serpent and of course, the most effective way to kill a serpent is to cut off its head. Our enemy is a spirit. To fight him, we must utilize the sword of the Spirit. This means that we cannot use carnal weapons; we need the power of the Holy Spirit.

All too often, believers find themselves being repeatedly attacked and bound by the Jezebel spirit because they are missing one or more pieces of God's armor. For example, it's not uncommon to see a believer who has the sword of the Spirit, the helmet of salvation, the shield of faith, the breastplate of righteousness and the belt of truth. However, the believer's feet is not covered with the gospel of peace because the believer is contentious, prideful and vengeful. They walk with the wrong people and keep heading in the wrong directions. When this happens, the believer is not fully covered. This allows the enemy to attack the believer by leading him or her into the wrong places.

Many believers don't study the Word often and for this reason, when under attack, they speak many religious words, but no true Word. Without knowledge of the Word, the believer will also be lacking in the faith arena. Additionally, this will take away the believer's peace because he or she doesn't have much Word to lean to. For this reason, the believer may find himself or herself defaulting to his or her flesh.
Proverbs 10:19 (ESV): *When words are many, transgression is not lacking, but whoever restrains his lips is prudent.*

We must be covered with the full armor of God if we want to effectively guard ourselves and our families from the Jezebel spirit and all of Satan's kingdom. Being religious isn't enough. Satan laughs at religion. Going to church every Sunday isn't enough. Satan goes to church everyday. Speaking in tongues and dancing for the Lord isn't enough. There is a such thing as false, demonic tongues. We need to wear the full armor of God to overcome our already defeated foe.

We're Trying to Fight Wearing the Wrong Armor

Before he became king, David found himself standing before a giant who was challenging Israel. That giant's name was Goliath. The Bible tells us that even King Saul was afraid of Goliath.

For forty days, Goliath would challenge Israel, demanding that an Israelite man come forth and fight him. He claimed that if the man could defeat him, the Philistines would serve Israel, but if the man could not defeat him, the Israelites were to serve Philistine. What you see here is a pagan nation trying to force God's people to serve them. This is an attempt to usurp the power of God. For this reason, the same spirit that was in the Philistines is the same spirit that we now refer to as Jezebel. As a matter of fact, the Philistines worshipped a pagan god (demon) named Dagon. Ironically, Dagon was believed to be the father of Baal (the principality that Jezebel served).

1 Samuel 17:12-39 (NIV): *Now David was the son of an*

Ephrathite named Jesse, who was from Bethlehem in Judah. Jesse had eight sons, and in Saul's time he was very old. Jesse's three oldest sons had followed Saul to the war: The firstborn was Eliab; the second, Abinadab; and the third, Shammah. David was the youngest. The three oldest followed Saul, but David went back and forth from Saul to tend his father's sheep at Bethlehem.

For forty days the Philistine came forward every morning and evening and took his stand.

Now Jesse said to his son David, "Take this ephah of roasted grain and these ten loaves of bread for your brothers and hurry to their camp. Take along these ten cheeses to the commander of their unit. See how your brothers are and bring back some assurance from them. They are with Saul and all the men of Israel in the Valley of Elah, fighting against the Philistines."

Early in the morning David left the flock in the care of a shepherd, loaded up and set out, as Jesse had directed. He reached the camp as the army was going out to its battle positions, shouting the war cry. Israel and the Philistines were drawing up their lines facing each other. David left his things with the keeper of supplies, ran to the battle lines and asked his brothers how they were. As he was talking with them, Goliath, the Philistine champion from Gath, stepped out from his lines and shouted his usual defiance, and David heard it. Whenever the Israelites saw the man, they all fled from him in great fear.

Now the Israelites had been saying, "Do you see how this man keeps coming out? He comes out to defy Israel. The king will give great wealth to the man who kills him. He will also give him his daughter in marriage and will exempt his family from taxes in Israel."

David asked the men standing near him, "What will be done for the man who kills this Philistine and removes this disgrace from Israel? Who is this uncircumcised Philistine that he should defy the armies of the living God?"

They repeated to him what they had been saying and told him, "This is what will be done for the man who kills him."

When Eliab, David's oldest brother, heard him speaking with the men, he burned with anger at him and asked, "Why have you come down here? And with whom did you leave those few sheep in the wilderness? I know how conceited you are and how wicked your heart is; you came down only to watch the battle."

"Now what have I done?" said David. "Can't I even speak?" He then turned away to someone else and brought up the same matter, and the men answered him as before. What David said was overheard and reported to Saul, and Saul sent for him.

David said to Saul, "Let no one lose heart on account of this Philistine; your servant will go and fight him."

Saul replied, "You are not able to go out against this Philistine and fight him; you are only a young man, and

he has been a warrior from his youth."
But David said to Saul, "Your servant has been keeping his father's sheep. When a lion or a bear came and carried off a sheep from the flock, I went after it, struck it and rescued the sheep from its mouth. When it turned on me, I seized it by its hair, struck it and killed it. Your servant has killed both the lion and the bear; this uncircumcised Philistine will be like one of them, because he has defied the armies of the living God. The LORD who rescued me from the paw of the lion and the paw of the bear will rescue me from the hand of this Philistine."
Saul said to David, "Go, and the LORD be with you."
Then Saul dressed David in his own tunic. He put a coat of armor on him and a bronze helmet on his head. David fastened on his sword over the tunic and tried walking around, because he was not used to them.
"I cannot go in these," he said to Saul, "because I am not used to them." So he took them off.

The armor that Saul gave to David represents carnality. It was designed to protect the warrior in a carnal war. For this reason, God did not want David to approach Goliath covered in natural armor. God wanted to prove Himself to His people and He wanted to teach them to trust Him. That's why He didn't allow David to get prepared for war. David thought he was going to the battle to deliver food to his brothers and their commander, but

God sent David to the battle to deliver His people. David went to the war completely unprepared for it, and that's what God wanted.

Once David decided to fight against Goliath, Saul had him clothed in the wrong armor. David removed that armor and decided to approach Goliath in faith; that was his armor.
1 Samuel 17:41-47 (ESV): *And the Philistine moved forward and came near to David, with his shield-bearer in front of him. And when the Philistine looked and saw David, he disdained him, for he was but a youth, ruddy and handsome in appearance. And the Philistine said to David, "Am I a dog, that you come to me with sticks?" And the Philistine cursed David by his gods. The Philistine said to David, "Come to me, and I will give your flesh to the birds of the air and to the beasts of the field." Then David said to the Philistine, "You come to me with a sword and with a spear and with a javelin, but I come to you in the name of the LORD of hosts, the God of the armies of Israel, whom you have defied. This day the LORD will deliver you into my hand, and I will strike you down and cut off your head. And I will give the dead bodies of the host of the Philistines this day to the birds of the air and to the wild beasts of the earth, that all the earth may know that there is a God in Israel, and that all this assembly may know that the LORD saves not with sword and spear. For*

the battle is the LORD's, and he will give you into our hand."

David, being a young man, had more faith than Saul and all of his army combined. He didn't trust his natural armor, so he took it off. This act was likely seen by his allies as foolish and prideful, but the truth was that David simply trusted God.

Sometimes, we try to approach Jezebel in our flesh or we try to approach it wearing the armor of religion, but not the whole armor of God. For this reason, we find ourselves in what appears to be a never-ending battle with the Jezebel spirit. To defeat Jezebel, we have to approach that spirit in the name of Jesus Christ; we cannot approach it carnally, nor can we defeat it with carnal weapons.
2 Corinthians 10:4 (KJV): *For the weapons of our warfare are not carnal, but mighty through God to the pulling down of strong holds.*

We're Bound by Our Brethren's Opinions of Us
Eliab, David's brother, became angry with him when he began to inquire about the prize.
1 Samuel 17:28 (ESV): *Now Eliab his eldest brother heard when he spoke to the men. And Eliab's anger was kindled against David, and he said, "Why have you come*

down? And with whom have you left those few sheep in the wilderness? I know your presumption and the evil of your heart, for you have come down to see the battle."
1 Samuel 17:31-33 (ESV): *When the words that David spoke were heard, they repeated them before Saul, and he sent for him. And David said to Saul, "Let no man's heart fail because of him. Your servant will go and fight with this Philistine." And Saul said to David, "You are not able to go against this Philistine to fight with him, for you are but a youth, and he has been a man of war from his youth."*

David had two people to discourage him: his brother and his leader. The same goes for many of us. Sometimes, our brothers and sisters in the Lord see us as mere, conceited youth with no power. The same goes for our leaders. Sometimes, a leader is blinded by what he or she sees in the natural. Sometimes, they are blinded by familiarity. When this happens, we find ourselves feeling like we can't defeat an already defeated foe: Satan. We then turn to the very people who keep running away from Goliath because we are being encouraged to trust in the people who appear to be wearing armor (religious robes, miters, and titles). Nevertheless, the power is in the name of Jesus Christ, not man.

What Eliab thought to be conceit was actually godly confidence. David was an early representative of the apostolic. When he saw Goliath boldly approaching God's people, like any true apostle, he burned with righteous indignation. The same happens today.

Confidence is oftentimes mistaken and mislabeled as pride and conceit by those who do not possess it. For example, a prideful man who's been in ministry for twenty years may see his armor bearer's confidence as foolish conceit and for this reason, he will likely rebuke him. The truth is ... what he's witnessing is not conceit; he is seeing a demonstration of unyielding faith. Since this is foreign to him, plus, he sees himself as "higher" than his armor-bearer, he will likely reprimand and rebuke the armor bearer. In some cases, he may even strip him of his position or excommunicate him from the church because the armor bearer is not carrying *his* armor (whatever he's clothing himself with, be it pride or a sense of entitlement). Instead, he himself is clothed in the full armor of God.

We Have Not Severed the Head of the Serpent

Satan and his demons are often represented by serpents. This is to help us understand not only how they attack, but how we are to attack them. Anytime, we find ourselves coming against a snake, we know to sever its head. Sure, there are many ways to kill a snake, but the most effective way is to decapitate it.

1 Samuel 17:48-51 (ESV): *When the Philistine arose and came and drew near to meet David, David ran quickly toward the battle line to meet the Philistine. And David put his hand in his bag and took out a stone and slung it and struck the Philistine on his forehead. The stone sank into his forehead, and he fell on his face to the ground. So David prevailed over the Philistine with a sling and with a stone, and struck the Philistine and killed him. There was no sword in the hand of David. Then David ran and stood over the Philistine and took his sword and drew it out of its sheath and killed him and cut off his head with it. When the Philistines saw that their champion was dead, they fled.*

David killed Goliath with a rock and an old-fashioned slingshot. Jesus Christ is our Rock and if we don't use Him, the Jezebel spirit will continue to haunt, attack and overcome us. David's choice to cut off Goliath's head was a representation of how we ought to fight the enemy. Additionally, before David cut off Goliath's head, he struck him on the head with a rock. The head represents the authority. Striking Goliath on the head with a rock is symbolic of us striking and overcoming Satan's head (authority) with the blood of Jesus. Cutting off Goliath's head is symbolic of destroying the works of the enemy. It represents removing the head (demonic authority) from the body (believers). How does this work? It means that we don't just defeat Jezebel for ourselves; we help other believers to war and overcome that spirit.

We are Submitted to the Wrong Leaders

Like most believers, David did not understand the mantle on his life. He was a humble servant of the Lord and he truly loved and respected Saul, his king. Nevertheless, God was setting David up to take Saul's place and Saul became jealous of him.

I have heard countless stories from believers who have suffered through or are suffering through what is commonly referred to as "church hurt." These believers love their leaders and feel compelled to serve them, even though their leaders have displayed jealousy and sometimes even hatred towards them. Nevertheless, the believers won't leave their leaders' covering simply because they believe that God sent them to that particular church. This causes them to be subject to the very Jezebel spirit that's trying to destroy them.

1 Samuel 18:6-11 (ESV): *As they were coming home, when David returned from striking down the Philistine, the women came out of all the cities of Israel, singing and dancing, to meet King Saul, with tambourines, with songs of joy, and with musical instruments. And the women sang to one another as they celebrated, "Saul has struck* *down his thousands, and David his ten thousands." And Saul was very angry, and this saying displeased him. He said, "They have ascribed to David ten thousands, and to me they have ascribed thousands, and what more can he have but the kingdom?" And Saul eyed David from that day on.*

The next day a harmful spirit from God rushed upon Saul, and he raved within his house while David was playing the lyre, as he did day by day. Saul had his spear in his hand. And Saul hurled the spear, for he thought, "I will pin David to the wall." But David evaded him twice.

David knew that Saul was trying to kill him, but because of legalism, David kept serving under Saul. He eventually fled from Saul when he realized that Saul would stop at nothing to take his life.

We Keep Getting Promoted by the Devil Who's Trying to Kill Us

One of the most common stories is: a leader does not like a believer and is always seeking to embarrass or harm that believer. Nevertheless, the believer believes that he was sent under his leader by God, so he refuses to leave. One day, the believer finally listens to God and decides to leave, but the enemy offers the believer a promotion in the very church that God told him to come out of. The believer takes the promotion and ends up extending his battle with Jezebel.

1 Samuel 18:12-16 (ESV): *Saul was afraid of David because the LORD was with him but had departed from Saul. So Saul removed him from his presence and made him a commander of a thousand. And he went out and came in before the people. And David had success in all his undertakings, for the LORD was with him. And when Saul saw that he had great success, he stood in fearful awe of him. But all Israel and Judah loved David, for he went out and came in before them.*

David knew that Saul hated him and wanted to take his life, yet and still, David wanted to impress Saul. He thought he could change Saul's mind about him, but he couldn't. By this time, Saul had an evil spirit in him, but he was still king of Israel. David acknowledged the king, but he did not want to *recognize* and acknowledge the devil that was in that king. Because of his respect and reverence of King Saul, David kept working directly under the man who was overly determined to kill him.

We Keep Romantically Engaging Ourselves with People Under Jezebel's Control

All too often, we underestimate how crafty the enemy is. All too often, we think that because the enemy isn't *outright* attacking us that he isn't attacking us *at all*. The reason for this is ... many believers understand war, but they do not understand warfare. War is a product of warfare. In war, armies physically fight with one another in an attempt to kill each other, but in warfare, a set of leaders come together and strategize. They come up with ideas as to how to kill the enemy, meaning, warfare is not physical; it's mental. We all know that the battle-ground that Satan fights us on is our minds. Nevertheless, this fact has become nothing but religious jargon to the average believer.

1 Samuel 18:17-20 (ESV): *Then Saul said to David, "Here is my elder daughter Merab. I will give her to you for a wife. Only be valiant for me and fight the LORD's battles." For Saul thought, "Let not my hand be against him, but let the hand of the Philistines be against him." And David said to Saul, "Who am I, and who are my relatives, my father's clan in Israel, that I should be son-in-law to the king?" But at the time when Merab, Saul's daughter, should have been given to David, she was given to Adriel the Meholathite for a wife.*

Now Saul's daughter Michal loved David. And they told Saul, and the thing pleased him. Saul thought, "Let me give her to him, that she may be a snare for him and that the hand of the Philistines may be against him." Therefore Saul said to David a second time, "You shall now be my son-in-law."

Before I married my second husband, Roger, I met the

family member who I spoke of earlier: Mara. Mara pretty much told me that Roger was her property and would do anything she told him to do. She didn't say this verbatim, but she did say that he considered her to be like his mother and if I had any problem with him, I needed to come to her. She told me that he would listen to her, but not me. God truly warned me and He opened the way of escape for me, but I did not take it.
1 Corinthians 10:13 (ESV): *No temptation has overtaken you that is not common to man. God is faithful, and he will not let you be tempted beyond your ability, but with the temptation he will also provide the way of escape, that you may be able to endure it.*

In order to marry Roger, according to his culture, I needed the approval of an older family member. Mara was that family member. She took a bus to Mississippi to examine my family. I was living with my Mom at the time because I was going through a divorce from my first husband. Again, I'd gone into sin because I'd made marriage an idol. When Mara came down to Mississippi, she didn't hide how controlling she was. Howbeit, she wasn't displaying angry aggression, so we (my family and I) brushed off her behavior as culture. She walked around my mother's house, going in the refrigerator whenever she wanted to and examining each room in the house. She even told my mother's live-in boyfriend that he needed to get a job. We laughed at her confrontational attitude and because I didn't like my mother's boyfriend, I applauded her behavior. Again, at that time, I was somewhat of a babe in Christ and I wasn't willing to wait on God to get whatever it was that I wanted.

When Mara left Mississippi, she called the rest of the family in Africa and gave her approval. I didn't know it at the time, but Mara approved me because she thought I was passive. *I wasn't.* I just displayed southern hospitality when she came to visit and I didn't argue with her about their cultural beliefs. At that time, Mara didn't tell me too much about their beliefs ... just the basics. But it was enough to let me know that I was not marrying into a God-fearing family; I was intermarrying with an unbeliever.

In Mara's mind, she'd given me a gift. She believed that I was forever indebted to her simply because she'd approved me to marry Roger. After I married Roger, Mara's controlling ways became more evident. I was determined to not be controlled by her but, at the same time, I tried to do whatever I could to stay on good terms with her. Not long after marrying Roger, I met Nancy (a pastor who'd stalked me) and not long after getting rid of Nancy, I met Mara's dark side. *Truthfully, I simply ac-*

knowledged her dark side. At first, I brushed off her behavior. I'd just gotten away from Nancy and there I was in the grips of that same spirit, only this time, it wasn't trying to enter my life religiously; it had come in romantically.

God warned me many times to walk away from Roger, but I did not adhere to His warnings, so when Mara started telling me, in so many words, that I was her property, I thought she was speaking from a cultural standpoint. I just thought it was mere words, so I didn't pay attention to the spiritual side of the matter. At that time, I was still relatively young in the faith.

After I married Roger, Mara told me that in their culture, I was the wife of the family. She explained to me that I was not only my husband's wife, but the family would refer to me as their wife. Of course, I wasn't going to perform wifely duties for the family; what she meant was ... I was the *property* of the family. The term "wife" denotes submission. It meant that the family was the head; they were to be my authority. I didn't realize what she was saying at the time, so I just proudly interrupted her, telling her about American culture. I thought I simply needed to remind her that I am American and I come from a different culture. Mara went on to refer to herself as my husband. After having a cultural debate with her, I decided to let Mara call herself whatever she wanted to call herself. I knew that I wasn't about to be controlled by her or their family, so I stopped debating and changed the topic of conversation.

During that marriage, I came to see the full effect of how much control Mara had over Roger. Honestly, I had never seen a human being under so much control in my life. Mara called our house several times a day in a wide variety of emotions. When I stopped talking with her, she started calling Roger's cell phone daily and talking about everything from their family to our marriage. She would often refer to me as "stupid" and whenever I asked him why he allowed her to talk so badly about me, he'd say, "That's just how she is."

The enemy simply wanted to monitor my life and use Roger as a snare. This is what happens with many believers who get married before they receive their identities from God. I didn't know who I was in Christ. I simply saw myself as a servant of God who wanted the American dream. What I didn't realize was that God had plans for me and the enemy was aware of those plans.

Once you romantically link yourself up to Jezebel or one of her Ahabs, Jezebel will watch to see if her plans to destroy you are effective. When they are proven ineffective, she will hate you all the more. At the same time, Ahab will begin to despise you and Jezebel will take Ahab back once she realizes that her weapon against you did not prosper.

1 Samuel 18:22-29 (ESV): *And Saul commanded his servants, "Speak to David in private and say, 'Behold, the king has delight in you, and all his servants love you. Now then become the king's son-in-law.'" And Saul's servants spoke those words in the ears of David. And David said, "Does it seem to you a little thing to become the king's son-in-law, since I am a poor man and have no reputation?" And the servants of Saul told him, "Thus and so did David speak." Then Saul said, "Thus shall you say to David, 'The king desires no bride-price except a hundred foreskins of the Philistines, that he may be avenged of the king's enemies.'" Now Saul thought to make David fall by the hand of the Philistines. And when his servants told David these words, it pleased David well to be the king's son-in-law. Before the time had expired, David arose and went, along with his men, and killed two hundred of the Philistines. And David brought their foreskins, which were given in full number to the king, that he might become the king's son-in-law. And Saul gave him his daughter Michal for a wife. But when Saul saw and knew that the* L*ORD* *was with David, and that Michal, Saul's daughter, loved him, Saul was even more afraid of David. So Saul was David's enemy continually.*

2 Samuel 6:16 (ESV): *As the ark of the LORD came into the city of David, Michal the daughter of Saul looked out of the window and saw King David leaping and dancing before the LORD, and she despised him in her heart.*

Michal is the equivalent of Ahab. Even though the Bible recounts that she initially loved David, it goes on to tell us that she eventually despised him. Such is the case of an unequally yoked relationship.

Whenever a believer tries to break away from the Baal principality, the enemy will send that believer a person who is either a Jezebel or is loyal to Jezebel. Understand this: anytime you marry one of Jezebel's Ahabs, you are *not* his wife or her husband. Spiritually speaking, Jezebel is married to Ahab and Ahab will always follow the instructions of Jezebel regarding you. You become the equivalent of a eunuch or a concubine. You will then witness firsthand the pain and the terror that Hagar was subjected to by Sarah. Even though Sarah didn't have the Jezebel spirit, she did have some jezebellic ways.

Genesis 16:1-6 (ESV): *Now Sarai Abram's wife bare him no children: and she had an handmaid, an Egyptian, whose name was Hagar. And Sarai said unto Abram, Behold now, the LORD hath restrained me from bearing: I pray thee, go in unto my maid; it may be that I may obtain children by her. And Abram hearkened to the voice of*

Sarai. And Sarai Abram's wife took Hagar her maid the Egyptian, after Abram had dwelt ten years in the land of Canaan, and gave her to her husband Abram to be his wife. And he went in unto Hagar, and she conceived: and when she saw that she had conceived, her mistress was despised in her eyes. And Sarai said unto Abram, My wrong be upon thee: I have given my maid into thy bosom; and when she saw that she had conceived, I was despised in her eyes: the LORD judge between me and thee. But Abram said unto Sarai, Behold, thy maid is in thy hand; do to her as it pleaseth thee. And when Sarai dealt hardly with her, she fled from her face.

We Keep Tolerating Jezebel

Leaders are inundated with emails from ahab'ed people who are not members of their churches. In these emails, the people cry out about their leaders' mistreatment of them, but when told to leave their churches, most people reply with, "God sent me here, so I can't leave yet." After this, the leaders don't hear from these people again until Jezebel attacks them again.

Many people are convinced that they are hearing from God when they are not. Because of this, they will sit under Jezebel's control and attempt to dodge every spear that Jezebel throws at them. They will justify sitting under their Sauls until they are successfully ahab'ed, successfully trained to become Jezebels or their leaders lose their positions (if this ever happens).

The same is true for leaders. Many leaders tolerate Jezebels because they are thirsty for the prophetic. They invite Jezebels to their churches, pay them to speak at their conferences and even allow these witches and warlocks to lay hands on them, making demonic impartations simply because they've witnessed what they believed to be a man or woman of God prophesying. They don't test the spirits or even pray about the people they invite into their churches or the people they ordain. Many see divination at work and think they are witnessing the power of God when, in truth, they are witnessing psychic powers in operation.
Revelation 2:20 (ESV): *But I have this against you, that you tolerate that woman Jezebel, who calls herself a prophetess and is teaching and seducing my servants to practice sexual immorality and to eat food sacrificed to idols.*
Exodus 7:20-22 (ESV): *Moses and Aaron did as the Lord commanded. In the sight of Pharaoh and in the sight of his servants he lifted up the staff and struck the water in the Nile, and all the water in the Nile turned into blood. And the fish in the Nile died, and the Nile stank, so that the Egyptians could not drink water from the Nile. There was blood throughout all the land of Egypt. But the magi-*

cians of Egypt did the same by their secret arts. So Pharaoh's heart remained hardened, and he would not listen to them, as the Lord had said.

Recently, a man who had been cross-dressing and calling himself a prophetess was exposed. The man was a transgendered male who changed his name in an attempt to disguise his identity. Even though he dressed, spoke and behaved as a woman, many of his male features were evident. This man had been invited to many churches and had prophesied over many of God's people. When exposed, the man publicly criticized the leader who'd exposed him and he claimed to have been born a hermaphrodite: a person born with both sexual organs. He'd not only been operating under a false name and the title of prophetess, he'd began to operate under the apostolic title.

What surprised (and disappointed) me was the number of people who came out in defense of the man ... *including* leaders. Truthfully, one would only need half of a mustard seed's amount of discernment to tell that he was truly a man. Not only did he have male features, but his mug shot was online from where he'd been arrested a few years prior. The mugshot displayed his name and gender, nevertheless, so many deceived believers came out in defense of him because they'd seen him prophesy.

This is the danger of the prophetic when used improperly. This is what happens when believers become so enthralled with and captivated by the prophetic that they disregard the Word of God and start chasing prophecies. Anytime this happens, believers will become desensitized and empathetic towards the Jezebel spirit and anyone who's operating in it. They will not only tolerate Jezebel, but they will defend Jezebel. When this happens, believers began to operate in the Zedekiah spirit, whereas, they will strike against true prophets and apostles of God in their attempts to defend Jezebel and her prophets.

1 Kings 22:19-25 (ESV): *And Micaiah said, "Therefore hear the word of the Lord: I saw the Lord sitting on his throne, and all the host of heaven standing beside him on his right hand and on his left; and the Lord said, 'Who will entice Ahab, that he may go up and fall at Ramoth-Gilead?' And one said one thing, and another said another. Then a spirit came forward and stood before the Lord, saying, 'I will entice him.' And the Lord said to him, 'By what means?' And he said, 'I will go out, and will be a lying spirit in the mouth of all his prophets.' And he said, 'You are to entice him, and you shall succeed; go out and do so.' Now therefore behold, the Lord has put a lying spirit in the mouth of all these your prophets; the Lord has declared disaster for you."*

Then Zedekiah the son of Chenaanah came near and

struck Micaiah on the cheek and said, "How did the Spirit of the Lord go from me to speak to you?" And Micaiah said, "Behold, you shall see on that day when you go into an inner chamber to hide yourself."

God exposed the man because the people who trusted in him were operating under a spirit of deception. Nevertheless, God made them knowledgeable about who and what he was; that way, they could no longer operate in the darkness. This is the same thing He did when He sent Elijah to confront Ahab. He used Elijah to expose Baal as a false god. After that, it was up to the people as to whether or not they wanted to follow God (thankfully they made the right choice) or continue following Baal. When this happened, following Baal would have no longer been a sin of ignorance; it would have been a sin of choice, otherwise, known as rebellion.

We are Not Utilizing Our Opportunities to Kill Jezebel

Legalism is one of the most effective satanic weapons in the church today. A legalist says, "Judge ye not," all the while, disregarding John 7:24 reads, "Do not judge by appearances, but judge with right judgment."

What is legalism? According to dictionary.com, legalism is: *strict adherence, or the principle of strict adherence, to law or prescription, especially to the letter rather than the spirit.* A legalist is a person who filters the Word of God through their lack of understanding, rather than leaning to God to get understanding. For this reason, a legalist will read a scripture and take it at face-value, meaning, the way the scripture reads, that's how they will accept it. The problem with this is ... there are parables in the Bible and there are mysteries that we can only understand through the Spirit of God.

Matthew 13:10-15 (ESV): *Then the disciples came and said to him, "Why do you speak to them in parables?" And he answered them, "To you it has been given to know the secrets of the kingdom of heaven, but to them it has not been given. For to the one who has, more will be given, and he will have an abundance, but from the one who has not, even what he has will be taken away. This is why I speak to them in parables, because seeing they do not see, and hearing they do not hear, nor do they understand. Indeed, in their case the prophecy of Isaiah is fulfilled that says: "You will indeed hear but never understand, and you will indeed see but never perceive." For this people's heart has grown dull, and with their ears they can barely hear, and their eyes they have closed, lest they should see with their eyes and hear with their ears and understand with their heart and turn, and I would heal them.*

In addition to strict adherence to the words on a page, a

legalist will follow his or her religious culture and combine it with the scriptures to create his or her own doctrine. Legalists are steadfast, stubborn, stiff-necked, and proud pseudo-intellectuals who pride themselves on being right, rather than being righteous. Some legalists, on the other hand, are men and women who love the Lord, but are bound by their interpretations of the Bible.

God gave David the opportunity to kill Saul two times, but because of legalism, David didn't take advantage of those opportunities. David reasoned within himself that Saul was an anointed man and for this reason, he would not touch him. Now, this sounds honorable to our natural mind, but in truth, God had delivered Saul to David. This means that it was okay for David to kill Saul.
1 Samuel 24:1-13 (ESV): *When Saul returned from following the Philistines, he was told, "Behold, David is in the wilderness of Engedi." Then Saul took three thousand chosen men out of all Israel and went to seek David and his men in front of the Wildgoats' Rocks. And he came to the sheepfolds by the way, where there was a cave, and Saul went in to relieve himself. Now David and his men were sitting in the innermost parts of the cave. And the men of David said to him, "Here is the day of which the Lord said to you, 'Behold, I will give your enemy into your hand, and you shall do to him as it shall seem good to you.'" Then David arose and stealthily cut off a corner of*

Saul's robe. And afterward David's heart struck him, because he had cut off a corner of Saul's robe. He said to his men, "The Lord forbid that I should do this thing to my lord, the Lord's anointed, to put out my hand against him, seeing he is the Lord's anointed." So David persuaded his men with these words and did not permit them to attack Saul. And Saul rose up and left the cave and went on his way.

Afterward David also arose and went out of the cave, and called after Saul, "My lord the king!" And when Saul looked behind him, David bowed with his face to the earth and paid homage. And David said to Saul, "Why do you listen to the words of men who say, 'Behold, David seeks your harm'? Behold, this day your eyes have seen how the Lord gave you today into my hand in the cave. And some told me to kill you, but I spared you. I said, 'I will not put out my hand against my lord, for he is the Lord's anointed.' See, my father, see the corner of your robe in my hand. For by the fact that I cut off the corner of your robe and did not kill you, you may know and see that there is no wrong or treason in my hands. I have not sinned against you, though you hunt my life to take it. May the Lord judge between me and you, may the Lord avenge me against you, but my hand shall not be against you.

This was David's first opportunity to kill Saul, but he used that opportunity to try and win Saul's favor and approval. This is commonly what we do as believers. We keep trying to prove ourselves to the people whose titles we respect and whose favor we want to earn. Like David, we even go so far as to tell the very Jezebels that are after us how we had the opportunity to hurt them but didn't take those opportunities. We even tell Jezebel that some of the people she's affiliated with has told us many times to leave her (or his) ministry and what those folks have said about Jezebel. This won't change Jezebel's mind about us. Not severing the head of the serpent only gives it another opportunity to come after us.

1 Samuel 26:1-20 (ESV): *Then David said to Ahimelech the Hittite, and to Joab's brother Abishai the son of Zeruiah, "Who will go down with me into the camp to Saul?" And Abishai said, "I will go down with you." So David and Abishai went to the army by night. And there lay Saul sleeping within the encampment, with his spear stuck in the ground at his head, and Abner and the army lay around him. Then Abishai said to David, "God has given your enemy into your hand this day. Now please let me pin him to the earth with one stroke of the spear, and I will not strike him twice." But David said to Abishai, "Do not destroy him, for who can put out his hand against the Lord's anointed and be guiltless?" And David said, "As the Lord lives, the Lord will strike him, or his day will come to die, or he will go down into battle and perish. The Lord* *forbid that I should put out my hand against the Lord's anointed. But take now the spear that is at his head and the jar of water, and let us go." So David took the spear and the jar of water from Saul's head, and they went away. No man saw it or knew it, nor did any awake, for they were all asleep, because a deep sleep from the Lord had fallen upon them.*

Then David went over to the other side and stood far off on the top of the hill, with a great space between them. And David called to the army, and to Abner the son of Ner, saying, "Will you not answer, Abner?" Then Abner answered, "Who are you who calls to the king?" And David said to Abner, "Are you not a man? Who is like you in Israel? Why then have you not kept watch over your lord the king? For one of the people came in to destroy the king your lord. This thing that you have done is not good. As the Lord lives, you deserve to die, because you have not kept watch over your lord, the Lord's anointed. And now see where the king's spear is and the jar of water that was at his head."

Saul recognized David's voice and said, "Is this your voice, my son David?" And David said, "It is my voice, my lord, O king." And he said, "Why does my lord pursue after his servant? For what have I done? What evil is on my hands? Now therefore let my lord the king hear the words of his servant. If it is the Lord who has stirred you up against me, may he accept an offering, but if it is men, may they be cursed before the Lord, for they have driven me out this day that I should have no share in the heritage of the Lord, saying, 'Go, serve other gods.' Now therefore, let not my blood fall to the earth away from the presence of the Lord, for the king of Israel has come out to seek a single flea like one who hunts a partridge in the mountains."

We are always trying to win the favor of the folks who are trying to destroy us. This doesn't make us more righteous in the eyes of God; this is nothing short of legalism and people-bondage. The way we destroy Jezebel is by confronting that spirit and of course, not being under its headship. The head represents authority, therefore, we cannot sit under Jezebel's ministry, claiming that God sent us there to destroy her or help her get delivered.

John 13:16 (ESV): *Truly, truly, I say to you, a servant is not greater than his master, nor is a messenger greater than the one who sent him.*

God sends people with the Jehu anointing to confront Jezebel. To come against a queen, God had to anoint Jehu as a king. Jehu was *anointed* to destroy Jezebel and to destroy Ahab's lineage. What does this mean? You are not a Jehu if you are sitting in Jezebel's church, eating from her religious doctrine. You are a eunuch with hopes of seeing her fall. Nevertheless, you may be the eunuch that pushes her from her wall when Jehu comes along and confronts Jezebel, but this does not mean it's God's will for you to sit under Jezebel.

There are many reasons that we find ourselves being pursued and continuously attacked by the Jezebel spirit, but we must always remember that we have been granted authority over the kingdom of darkness through the blood of Jesus Christ.
Luke 10:17-19 (ESV): *The seventy-two returned with joy, saying, "Lord, even the demons are subject to us in your name!" And he said to them, "I saw Satan fall like lightning from heaven. Behold, I have given you authority to tread on serpents and scorpions, and over all the power of the enemy, and nothing shall hurt you.*

The point is: once you know the condition of a person, you need to find out what that person's condition leads him or her to do. We all know what Jezebel's condition leads her to do, so why sit under her and claim to be the one God sent to destroy her? A "sent one" is an apostle and apostles are sent to dismantle and destroy the works of the enemy. An apostle is *never* sent to glean from a witch.

CHAPTER 5

Cleaning the Courts

In Volume I of Jezebellion, we discussed the three dimensions of the mind. They are the conscious, subconscious, and the unconscious mind. The first layer is the conscious mind. This is the part of the mind that responds to what you're currently seeing, hearing, touching, smelling or tasting. It deals with the present. Next, there's the subconscious mind. The subconscious mind is where you store memories, beliefs, and habits. It responds to the present but stores information from the past. The last dimension is the unconscious mind. This is the part of the mind that affects us without our permission. It is responsible for breathing and it controls our instinctual responses. This is the part of our minds that the enemy cannot access. If he could, he'd be able to shut down the breath of God from within us.

Because the enemy knows he cannot access the unconscious mind of a believer, he works tirelessly to get as close to that part of our hearts as possible. Our subconscious has three levels with each level advancing to wards the unconscious mind. Satan wants to get as close to the unconscious mind as possible. In the third level of our hearts, we store whatever it is that we have received as truth. In the second level, we store what we have received as facts. Satan's goal is to get us to place facts above truth; that way, he can filter the truth through our fact-filter. This means that if something does not make sense to our natural reasoning, we will no longer receive it. This is what the Bible refers to as exchanging the truth for a lie. Please see the charts below.

Unconscious	**Functions**
	Controls Breathing
	Stores Forgotten Trauma
	Inaccessible to Demons

Subconscious	**Functions (by Level)**
Level Three	Gateway for I Am
	Stores Truth
	Stores Memories (Memory Recall)
	Stores Religious Beliefs
	Houses Established Beliefs
	Heart
Level Two	Entrance to Heart

	Decision Making Center Stores Facts and Secular Beliefs Houses Emotions Stores New Music
Level One	Waiting Room for Level Two Undecided Information New Information Stores Gossip

Conscious	**Functions**
	Windows to Soul
	Waiting Room for Subconscious
	Present Information
	Undecided Information

The conscious represents the doorway. For example, when someone walks up to you and starts talking to you, they are engaging your conscious mind. Now, if you're familiar with and trust the person you are engaging with, even though that person is engaging your conscious mind, he or she still has direct access to your subconscious. That's because the information being shared with you no longer is being tested by you because of familiarity. This is why God tells us to guard our hearts. He goes on to say that the issues of life flow from our hearts (Proverbs 4:23).

Soul ties give people direct access to your heart and the more intimate you are with a person, the greater degree of access they have to you. For example, your distant cousin doesn't have access to the same level of your heart as your best friend has. That's because even though you're related to your cousin, he or she is distant and, therefore, anything the cousin says to you will not be immediately received by you. Instead, you'll store it in the doorway of your subconscious and test it. For this reason, the enemy wants to get people in your life that he can get as close to your heart as possible. He doesn't want you to have casual friendships because that limits his access to you. Instead, he wants you to have "best friends" and intimate romantic relationships (boyfriends or girlfriends) with the people he sends your way. If he successfully pulls this off, he can access your heart. It's pretty similar to a scene in your favorite spy movie where the star wears a costume so that he can access a high-security area. He puts on a wig, changes his voice and alters the way he walks so that he can look like someone the guard is somewhat familiar with. If this works, he's able to get past the guard and access the control center. This is the same thing demons do. They access the heart of people and use those people to become familiar acquaintances in your life. The enemy then has those people to open up to you so that you'll feel comfortable opening up to them. Basically, the enemy is trying to breach your security. If you don't guard your heart like the Word tells you to do, your new "best friend" or "lover" will get past your discernment and from there, the enemy will create a soul tie between you and that person. This soul tie represents a rope that allows the enemy to cross over from one person's heart into the heart of the next person. From there, the enemy will begin to attack all godly and relevant information so that he can make his way from the first level of the subconscious towards the third level of the subconscious. If he successfully enters the third level, he will destroy your relationship with God one question at a time. He'll ask, "Did God really say that?" or "Is that what God really meant?" Before long, you will begin to question the truth and when this happens, Satan will introduce you to lies disguised as facts. If he can get you to exchange the truth for a lie, he can attack your relationship with God. This is his way of trying to remove your covering. If he is successful, he will then begin to use you to spread the lies that you have in your heart and once he's done with you, he'll discard you. The Jezebel spirit is the perfect demon for this job because Jezebel specializes in creating soul ties.

I used to always wonder why the people who entered my life were so quick to label me as their "best friend." A few months or a few years later, I would watch God drive those same folks away from me after, of course, I'd accepted that they were never my friends to begin with. I foolishly chose the path of experience, rather than receiving the wisdom of God through His Word and through wise counsel. Because I chose the path of experience, I wasted many years getting wisdom that I could have gotten in a matter of weeks or months. Nevertheless, even though my path to the truth was long and rocky, it was the path that I had to take because I needed deliverance, but I was too ignorant and too prideful to seek it. I came to realize that the enemy is not at all patient. For this reason, God tells us to be patient. You see, when we're patient, we provoke the enemy to come out of hiding. This is the reason many singles find themselves constantly meeting folks who want to rush into relationships. They say, "I love you" when they don't know what or, better yet, who love is. They say, "God said that you are my wife (or husband)," when they have not heard from God. They say, "I dreamed about our first child," when their dreams came from the realm of divination and not from God. They want to rush into a soul tie because again, the enemy is impatient. Patience is a fruit of the Holy Spirit and if we embrace patience and all of God's fruit, it'll be easier for us to avoid Jezebel

and every other demon Satan assigns to our lives.
Galatians 5:22-23 (ESV): *But the fruit of the Spirit is love, joy, peace, patience, kindness, goodness, faithfulness, gentleness, self-control; against such things there is no law.*

Cleaning the courts of our hearts involves us making the fruit of the Holy Spirit a part of our daily lives. We start by applying this fruit to every relationship we are currently in. Like I said before, when you start to do this, you force the enemy to come out of hiding. That is, if you do it consistently and without fail. It can't be a trial; it has to be a new lifestyle.

Next, you start cleaning the outer courts by monitoring what you allow into your ear-gates and your eye-gates. This is important because if there are any demonic spirits operating in you, they are feeding themselves through your relationships and whatever you use to entertain yourself. For example, have you ever had one of those days where you could only seem to think of negative things? On that particular day, you seem to drift from one negative thought to the next. In many cases when this happens, you're basically dealing with a demon that feeds on negativity, so to gather strength, it will start to cloud your mind with negative thoughts. It wants you to become angry with the folks who've hurt you and it wants you to slander, backbite and talk about anyone who's disappointed you. The way to combat this is to pray for the people who've hurt or disappointed you and to begin to praise God. What you're doing is attacking an already weak spirit.

Matthew 5:44-45 (ESV): *But I say to you, Love your enemies and pray for those who persecute you, so that you may be sons of your Father who is in heaven. For he makes his sun rise on the evil and on the good, and sends rain on the just and on the unjust.*

Luke 6:27-31 (ESV): *But I say to you who hear, Love your enemies, do good to those who hate you, bless those who curse you, pray for those who abuse you. To one who strikes you on the cheek, offer the other also, and from one who takes away your cloak do not withhold your tunic either. Give to everyone who begs from you, and from one who takes away your goods do not demand them back. And as you wish that others would do to you, do so to them.*

Stop watching movies that feed the death in you and only watch shows and movies that help you to grow spiritually and financially. Next, stop listening to demonic music or music that feeds your sinful nature. Listen to music that builds up your spirit man and gives glory to God. Lastly, surround yourself with wise people and don't get personally involved with foolish or rebellious people. Monitor what goes in your heart by monitoring who has access to your heart!

Proverbs 13:20 (ESV): *Whoever walks with the wise becomes wise, but the companion of fools will suffer harm.*

To cleanse the second level (subconscious), you may have to go through deliverance. Additionally, cleansing this level is like cleaning out a closet. Ask the Lord to reveal what's hiding in your heart and begin to confront everything that's unlike God. Renounce ungodly beliefs and start getting as much Word in you as possible. Go through old doctrinal beliefs and start testing them by comparing them with the Word of God. Anytime you find anything that is not from God, renounce it and sever your ties with it. Additionally, ask the Lord to give you a new heart and a new mind.

Finally, begin to war for your freedom. The enemy is worse than a jilted lover; he doesn't let go easily, nor will he give up easily. You have to be more determined to receive and maintain your freedom than he is to take it away from you. If Jezebel is more persistent than you are, she will attack you until you submit to her. Don't give in. Utilize your God-given authority and decapitate that demon every time it raises up its head in your life. When Jezebel came after me, it was persistent and it threatened to take away everything I had if I did not give in to its wicked desires. Nevertheless, to maintain my freedom, I was willing to give up *everything* I had. This means that the enemy could not find anything to hold over my head. When I was faced with the threat of losing my good name, I told the enemy that God would give me a new name like He did with Abraham (formerly Abram), Sarah (formerly Sarai), Israel (formerly Jacob), Peter (formerly Simon), and Paul (formerly Saul). When I was faced with the threat of losing everything I'd worked for, I reminded the enemy that the earth is the Lord's and the fullness thereof. I also looked around my house and my life to see what I'd received as a reward for my sins or an incentive to sin. I started throwing all of that stuff away. When the enemy threatened my friendships, I told him that deliverance is the children's bread. He didn't realize it, but he was threatening to deliver me and I saw it for what it was. I then started asking the Lord to close every demonic access door that was open in my life and to drive away any friends who He had not sent into my life. When the enemy held my marriage over my head, I reminded him that God called me to peace, therefore, if the unbeliever wanted to leave, it was my responsibility to let him leave. I also repented for marrying without God's permission and I started transferring the love that belonged to God back to Him; that way, I could love the man I was married to the way God wanted me to love him and not in an idolatrous way. I also prayed for a heart of submission. What I didn't realize was that by submitting to my ex, I was moving out of God's way and letting Him deliver me from the Egypt that I'd placed myself in. By doing so, God blessed me to lead my ex through the sinner's prayer while we were going through a divorce! I obeyed God and because of that, Roger got saved. It was too late for us, but it was not too late for him to make a fresh start with Jesus. When the enemy threatened my life, I reminded him that my life was not my own; I went and died to myself. How did he respond? He had no choice but to get behind me and take back everything he'd placed in my life. One of the most dangerous things you can do is place so much value in some thing or some person that the enemy has the ability to effectively get you to bow down to him by threatening to take that thing or that person away from you. That difficult childhood I talked about ended up serving as a blessing because I learned earlier on in life that I would survive without the stuff and the people. I learned that with every wound, I would eventually heal, so the enemy's attacks backfired. Little did he know, he was training a warrior who would someday take what she learned and turn it against him. I stopped being the victim and I started taking accountability for my own actions.

Understand this: Jezebel's strength in your life is determined by the sin you're in. Sin gets in by causing you to value things, ideas and people over the Word of God. Ask the Lord to deliver you from people bondage, people pleasing, idolatry, and the love of things. When the enemy looks around to see if there is anything or anyone he can hold over your head, he should only see Jesus. Since he cannot touch Jesus, he will flee from you because placing your relationship with God above all things renders the enemy powerless in your life. It also allows God to send the right people into your life and to give you every desire of your heart because those desires and people aren't misplaced; they aren't sitting on God's throne in your heart.

Go throughout the courts of your heart and do some cleaning. Do this as often as you can so that you can continue to maintain your freedom. Know this: you can't lose unless you refuse to win. Jesus Christ has already gotten the victory, so as long as you stay in Him, you too will have the victory through Him.

CHAPTER 6

Rules of Engagement

It is imperative that we understand governmental authority when confronting the Jezebel spirit. The reason for this is ... demons understand governmental authority and will play by the rules when you don't know them. That's because playing by the rules gives them an advantage over a person who lacks knowledge. At the same time, there are certain rules that demons cannot and will not violate. For example, a high-ranking demon will not and cannot attack someone of low-standing because by doing so, it violates the rules of engagement.

Isaiah 59:19 (ESV): *So shall they fear the name of the LORD from the west, and his glory from the rising of the sun. When the enemy shall come in like a flood, the Spirit of the LORD shall lift up a standard against him.*

The Greek word for "standard" is "kanón." According to Strong's Concordance, it means: (lit: a level, ruler), a rule, regulation, rule of conduct or doctrine, (b) a measured (defined) area, province. There are rules of en gagement that must be followed in the arena of warfare. For example, Jezebel violated the rules of engagement many times, but one of those violations was her attack against and murder of Naboth. Naboth didn't stand a chance against Jezebel and Jezebel knew this. She used her position as queen to have an innocent man murdered simply because he'd said "no" to giving away his inheritance.

1 Kings 21:1-24 (ESV): *Now Naboth the Jezreelite had a vineyard in Jezreel, beside the palace of Ahab king of Samaria. And after this Ahab said to Naboth, "Give me your vineyard, that I may have it for a vegetable garden, because it is near my house, and I will give you a better vineyard for it; or, if it seems good to you, I will give you its value in money." But Naboth said to Ahab, "The Lord forbid that I should give you the inheritance of my fathers." And Ahab went into his house vexed and sullen because of what Naboth the Jezreelite had said to him, for he had said, "I will not give you the inheritance of my fathers." And he lay down on his bed and turned away his face and would eat no food.*

But Jezebel his wife came to him and said to him, "Why is your spirit so vexed that you eat no food?" And he said to her, "Because I spoke to Naboth the Jezreelite and said to him, 'Give me your vineyard for money, or else, if it please you, I will give you another vineyard for it.' And he answered, 'I will not give you my vineyard.'" And Jezebel his wife said to him, "Do you now govern Israel? Arise and eat bread and let your heart be cheerful; I will give you the vineyard of Naboth the Jezreelite."

So she wrote letters in Ahab's name and sealed them with his seal, and she sent the letters to the elders and the leaders who lived with Naboth in his city. And she wrote in the letters, "Proclaim a fast, and set Naboth at the head of the people. And set two worthless men opposite him, and let them bring a charge against him, saying, 'You have cursed God and the king.' Then take him out and stone him to death." And the men of his city, the elders and the leaders who lived in his city, did as Jezebel had sent word to them. As it was written in the letters that she had sent to them, they proclaimed a fast and set Naboth at the head of the people. And the two worthless men came in and sat opposite him. And the worthless men brought a charge against Naboth in the presence of the people, saying, "Naboth cursed God and the king." So they took him outside the city and stoned him to death with stones. Then they sent to Jezebel, saying, "Naboth has been stoned; he is dead."

As soon as Jezebel heard that Naboth had been stoned and was dead, Jezebel said to Ahab, "Arise, take possession of the vineyard of Naboth the Jezreelite, which he refused to give you for money, for Naboth is not alive, but dead." And as soon as Ahab heard that Naboth was dead, Ahab arose to go down to the vineyard of Naboth the Jezreelite,

to take possession of it.
Then the word of the Lord came to Elijah the Tishbite, saying, "Arise, go down to meet Ahab king of Israel, who is in Samaria; behold, he is in the vineyard of Naboth, where he has gone to take possession. And you shall say to him, 'Thus says the Lord, "Have you killed and also taken possession?"' And you shall say to him, 'Thus says the Lord: "In the place where dogs licked up the blood of Naboth shall dogs lick your own blood."'"
Ahab said to Elijah, "Have you found me, O my enemy?" He answered, "I have found you, because you have sold yourself to do what is evil in the sight of the Lord. Behold, I will bring disaster upon you. I will utterly burn you up, and will cut off from Ahab every male, bond or free, in Israel. And I will make your house like the house of Jeroboam the son of Nebat, and like the house of Baasha the son of Ahijah, for the anger to which you have provoked me, and because you have made Israel to sin. And of Jezebel the Lord also said, 'The dogs shall eat Jezebel within the walls of Jezreel.' Anyone belonging to Ahab who dies in the city the dogs shall eat, and anyone of his who dies in the open country the birds of the heavens shall eat."

The murder of Naboth was a crime that, in itself, would have provoked the Lord to anger but, at the same time, it wasn't the only violation. Again, Jezebel violated protocol because she'd attacked a defenseless man. This was bullying; it was a misuse of power. For example, in our modern day government, there are public international laws regarding war and warfare. One such law is found in Article 42 (Occupants of aircraft) within the Protocols Additional to the Geneva Conventions of 12 August 1949, and it reads:

> Article 42 — Occupants of aircraft
>
> 1. No person parachuting from an aircraft in distress shall be made the object of attack during his descent.
>
> 2. Upon reaching the ground in territory controlled by an adverse Party, a person who has parachuted from an aircraft in distress shall be given an opportunity to surrender before being made the object of attack, unless it is apparent that he is engaging in a hostile act.
>
> 3. Airborne troops are not protected by this Article.

Many of the laws of old as well as the modern day laws prohibit the excessive use of power. During war, when a military official misuses his or her power, that official is likely to be accused of committing war crimes and may be brought up on charges.

By taking possession of Naboth's vineyard, Ahab was in

violation of several of the Ten Commandments, which were the laws of the land at that time. Not only were Ahab and Jezebel guilty of Naboth's death, but they were also guilty of violating the law regarding the disposition of property. Even after Naboth's death, his vineyard was supposed to remain in his family. That's why God sent Elijah to say to Ahab, "Thus says the Lord, 'Have you killed and also taken possession?'" Jezebel and Ahab were both guilty of violating several of the Ten Commandments. They include:

- **"Thou shalt not take the name of the LORD thy God in vain: for the LORD will not hold him guiltless that taketh his name in vain" (Deuteronomy 5:11).** Using God's name in vain is much more than coupling it with profanity. It also means to use God's name in any way that brings dishonor to Him. This includes saying the Lord said something that He did not say (false prophecies). Jezebel had two scoundrels to say that Naboth cursed God as well as the king. Now, we do know that Jezebel worshiped Baal, but she used the name of the God of Israel for her accusation. This was using God's name in vain.
- **"You shall not kill" (Deuteronomy 5:17).** Jezebel had Naboth killed so that she could gain possession of his vineyard.

- **"Neither shall you steal" (Deuteronomy 5:19).** Even after Naboth's death, the vineyard was supposed to remain in Naboth's family. By taking possession of the vineyard, Jezebel and Ahab were guilty of theft.
- **"Neither shall you bear false witness against your neighbor" (Deuteronomy 5:20).** Jezebel had two scoundrels to lie on Naboth. This was what the bible refers to as "bearing false witness."
- **"Neither shall you desire your neighbor's wife, neither shall you covet your neighbor's house, his field, or his manservant, or his maidservant, his ox, or his donkey, or anything that is your neighbor's" (Deuteronomy 5:21).** Ahab coveted Naboth's field and this covetous led to one of the most heinous crimes during Ahab's reign and that is: Naboth's death.

Jezebel and Ahab didn't just bully Naboth; they killed him. They were also guilty of bullying God's prophets. The same is true for the Jezebel-Ahab duo to this day. There are many people in leadership, not just in the corporate world, but also in the church, who use their positions to bully others. As a matter of fact, Jezebel was nothing but a bully. Notice that Ahab hated and bullied the prophets of God, but he did not rise against Jehoshaphat, the king of Judah. Jehoshaphat was a man of God. Why didn't Ahab try to have him killed? The answer is simple. Jehoshaphat was a king and as such, he had the legal right to declare war against Ahab. Ahab preferred to target people who could not legally oppose him. Again, demons will violate whatever rules they can violate. By killing Naboth, Ahab provoked God to wrath.

Since Jehoshaphat was a compromised king, meaning, he allied himself with Ahab, God could not use Jehoshaphat to wage war against the household of Ahab. God is a God of order, so He had a prophet to go and anoint another man as king. He had Jehu anointed as king because the only person who could legally attack a king was another king.

2 Kings 9:1-13 (ESV): *Then Elisha the prophet called one of the sons of the prophets and said to him, "Tie up your garments, and take this flask of oil in your hand, and go to Ramoth-gilead. And when you arrive, look there for Jehu the son of Jehoshaphat, son of Nimshi. And go in and have him rise from among his fellows, and lead him to an inner chamber. Then take the flask of oil and pour it on his head and say, 'Thus says the LORD, I anoint you king over Israel.' Then open the door and flee; do not linger."*
So the young man, the servant of the prophet, went to

Ramoth-gilead. And when he came, behold, the commanders of the army were in council. And he said, "I have a word for you, O commander." And Jehu said, "To which of us all?" And he said, "To you, O commander." So he arose and went into the house. And the young man poured the oil on his head, saying to him, "Thus says the Lord*, the God of Israel, I anoint you king over the people of the* Lord*, over Israel. And you shall strike down the house of Ahab your master, so that I may avenge on Jezebel the blood of my servants the prophets, and the blood of all the servants of the* Lord*. For the whole house of Ahab shall perish, and I will cut off from Ahab every male, bond or free, in Israel. And I will make the house of Ahab like the house of Jeroboam the son of Nebat, and like the house of Baasha the son of Ahijah. And the dogs shall eat Jezebel in the territory of Jezreel, and none shall bury her." Then he opened the door and fled.*

When Jehu came out to the servants of his master, they said to him, "Is all well? Why did this mad fellow come to you?" And he said to them, "You know the fellow and his talk." And they said, "That is not true; tell us now." And he said, "Thus and so he spoke to me, saying, 'Thus says the Lord*, I anoint you king over Israel.'" Then in haste every man of them took his garment and put it under him on the bare steps, and they blew the trumpet and proclaimed, "Jehu is king."*

Nevertheless, by the time Jehu became king, Ahab was already dead. There's a reason for this and it is ... to rid the land of Jezebel and her whoredoms, God first needed to remove the crown from Jezebel's head. Ahab represented that crown because he was the one who authorized her. What does this mean for us? It means that in order to confront Jezebel, we first need to confront and overcome Ahab. Now, this does not mean that we are to kill any man or woman operating as an Ahab. It does mean that when dealing with legal authorities, the proper order is to confront the head of the home because he is the one authorized by God to run that home.

Ahab was the king and if God had simply gotten rid of Jezebel, Ahab would have done something most of us have witnessed people with the Ahab spirit do today: he would have went and found himself another Jezebel. This is why it is error for people to try to talk an ahab'ed soul into leaving his or her Jezebel. The person needs deliverance from the Ahab spirit and every other spirit that is inhabiting that person. Anytime a woman (for example) who has the Jezebel spirit leaves her ahab'ed lover or passes away, the ahab'ed soul will look for another woman who is similar to the one he lost. If you introduce him to a kind, godly woman, he will not be happy or content with her. Instead, he will reject the woman, or if he enters a relationship with her, he will likely cheat on her for someone who has the Jezebel spirit. This is because Ahab is married to Jezebel and until the man gets delivered, he will not stop seeking Jezebel. Sure, queen Jezebel was a huge problem, but her husband was a problem as well. He'd authorized the wicked Jezebel to operate as queen over God's people and then, he stood by and watched her kill off God's prophets one by one. God needed to remove Jezebel's license to operate and that license was a passive, weak king by the name of Ahab. To do this, God allowed the very spirit that Ahab trusted to deceive him into going to war against Ramoth-Gilead.

1 Kings 22:13-23 (ESV): *And the messenger who went to summon Micaiah said to him, "Behold, the words of the prophets with one accord are favorable to the king. Let your word be like the word of one of them, and speak favorably." But Micaiah said, "As the Lord lives, what the Lord says to me, that I will speak." And when he had come to the king, the king said to him, "Micaiah, shall we go to Ramoth-gilead to battle, or shall we refrain?" And he answered him, "Go up and triumph; the Lord will give it into the hand of the king." But the king said to him, "How many times shall I make you swear that you speak to me nothing but the truth in the name of the Lord?" And he said, "I saw all Israel scattered on the mountains, as sheep that have no shepherd. And the Lord said, 'These have no master; let each return to his home in peace.'"*

And the king of Israel said to Jehoshaphat, "Did I not tell you that he would not prophesy good concerning me, but evil?" And Micaiah said, "Therefore hear the word of the Lord: I saw the Lord sitting on his throne, and all the host of heaven standing beside him on his right hand and on his left; and the Lord said, 'Who will entice Ahab, that he may go up and fall at Ramoth-gilead?' And one said one thing, and another said another. Then a spirit came forward and stood before the Lord, saying, 'I will entice him.' And the Lord said to him, 'By what means?' And he said, 'I will go out, and will be a lying spirit in the mouth of all his prophets.' And he said, 'You are to entice him, and you shall succeed; go out and do so.' Now therefore behold, the Lord has put a lying spirit in the mouth of all these your prophets; the Lord has declared disaster for you."

1 Kings 22:29-38 (ESV): *So the king of Israel and Jehoshaphat the king of Judah went up to Ramoth-gilead. And the king of Israel said to Jehoshaphat, "I will disguise myself and go into battle, but you wear your robes." And the king of Israel disguised himself and went into battle. Now the king of Syria had commanded the thirty-two captains of his chariots, "Fight with neither small nor great, but only with the king of Israel." And when the captains of the chariots saw Jehoshaphat, they said, "It is surely the king of Israel." So they turned to fight against him. And Jehoshaphat cried out. And when the captains of the chariots saw that it was not the king of Israel, they*

turned back from pursuing him. But a certain man drew his bow at random and struck the king of Israel between the scale armor and the breastplate. Therefore he said to the driver of his chariot, "Turn around and carry me out of the battle, for I am wounded." And the battle continued that day, and the king was propped up in his chariot facing the Syrians, until at evening he died. And the blood of the wound flowed into the bottom of the chariot. And about sunset a cry went through the army, "Every man to his city, and every man to his country!"
So the king died, and was brought to Samaria. And they buried the king in Samaria. And they washed the chariot by the pool of Samaria, and the dogs licked up his blood, and the prostitutes washed themselves in it, according to the word of the Lord that he had spoken.

Before confronting Jezebel, Ahab had to first be warned, then judged, and finally, that judgment was carried out.
Ezekiel 3:17-19 (ESV): *Son of man, I have made you a watchman for the house of Israel. Whenever you hear a word from my mouth, you shall give them warning from me. If I say to the wicked, 'You shall surely die,' and you give him no warning, nor speak to warn the wicked from his wicked way, in order to save his life, that wicked person shall die for his iniquity, but his blood I will require at your hand. But if you warn the wicked, and he does not turn from his wickedness, or from his wicked way, he shall*

die for his iniquity, but you will have delivered your soul.

Ahab was warned several times, but he chose to continue tolerating Jezebel and promoting Baal worship. For this reason, God judged him and then, He proceeded to carry out that judgment using a man named Jehu. Jehu was anointed to destroy the house of Ahab. Why was this? Why wasn't the king simply impeached? Impeachment didn't exist back then. When a man was king, he would live and die as a king and then, the kingdom would go to his eldest son. Ahab's sons were wicked just like their father and their mother. God needed to purge Israel of Ahab and Jezebel. This was a picture of deliverance taking place.

2 Kings 9:14-37 (ESV): *Thus Jehu the son of Jehoshaphat the son of Nimshi conspired against Joram. (Now Joram with all Israel had been on guard at Ramoth-gilead against Hazael king of Syria, but King Joram had returned to be healed in Jezreel of the wounds that the Syrians had given him, when he fought with Hazael king of Syria.) So Jehu said, "If this is your decision, then let no one slip out of the city to go and tell the news in Jezreel." Then Jehu mounted his chariot and went to Jezreel, for Joram lay there. And Ahaziah king of Judah had come down to visit Joram.*

Now the watchman was standing on the tower in Jezreel, and he saw the company of Jehu as he came and said, "I see a company." And Joram said, "Take a horseman and send to meet them, and let him say, 'Is it peace?'" So a man on horseback went to meet him and said, "Thus says the king, 'Is it peace?'" And Jehu said, "What do you have to do with peace? Turn around and ride behind me." And the watchman reported, saying, "The messenger reached them, but he is not coming back." Then he sent out a second horseman, who came to them and said, "Thus the king has said, 'Is it peace?'" And Jehu answered, "What do you have to do with peace? Turn around and ride behind me." Again the watchman reported, "He reached them, but he is not coming back. And the driving is like the driving of Jehu the son of Nimshi, for he drives furiously."

Joram said, "Make ready." And they made ready his chariot. Then Joram king of Israel and Ahaziah king of Judah set out, each in his chariot, and went to meet Jehu, and met him at the property of Naboth the Jezreelite. And when Joram saw Jehu, he said, "Is it peace, Jehu?" He answered, "What peace can there be, so long as the whorings and the sorceries of your mother Jezebel are so many?" Then Joram reined about and fled, saying to Ahaziah, "Treachery, O Ahaziah!" And Jehu drew his bow with his full strength, and shot Joram between the shoulders, so that the arrow pierced his heart, and he sank in his chariot. Jehu said to Bidkar his aide, "Take him up and throw him on the plot of ground belonging to Naboth the Jezreelite. For remember, when you and I rode side by side behind Ahab his father, how the LORD made this pronouncement against him: 'As surely as I saw yesterday the blood of Naboth and the blood of his sons—declares the LORD—I will repay you on this plot of ground.' Now therefore take him up and throw him on the plot of ground, in accordance with the word of the LORD."

When Ahaziah the king of Judah saw this, he fled in the direction of Beth-haggan. And Jehu pursued him and said, "Shoot him also." And they shot him in the chariot at the ascent of Gur, which is by Ibleam. And he fled to Megiddo and died there. His servants carried him in a chariot to Jerusalem, and buried him in his tomb with his fathers in the city of David.

In the eleventh year of Joram the son of Ahab, Ahaziah began to reign over Judah.

When Jehu came to Jezreel, Jezebel heard of it. And she painted her eyes and adorned her head and looked out of the window. And as Jehu entered the gate, she said, "Is it peace, you Zimri, murderer of your master?" And he lifted up his face to the window and said, "Who is on my side? Who?" Two or three eunuchs looked out at him. He said, "Throw her down." So they threw her down. And some of her blood spattered on the wall and on the horses, and they trampled on her. Then he went in and ate and drank. And he said, "See now to this cursed woman and bury her, for she is a king's daughter." But when they went to bury her, they found no more of her than the skull and the feet and the palms of her hands. When they came back and told him, he said, "This is the word of the LORD, *which he spoke by his servant Elijah the Tishbite: 'In the territory of Jezreel the dogs shall eat the flesh of Jezebel, and the corpse of Jezebel shall be as dung on the face of the field in the territory of Jezreel, so that no one can say, This is Jezebel.'"*

After Ahab was killed, a couple of his sons were killed and then, his wife Jezebel was killed. When dealing with demonic networks, the strongman is often bound first and then, the rest of the spirits can easily be cast out. Ahab was the strongman. This is why so many people unsuccessfully wage war against Jezebel. They forget to confront, bind, and cast out Ahab! To confront Ahab means to warn the person who's operating in the Ahab spirit and then, if that person does not repent, he needs to be removed from authority. Of course, he will fight his removal, but there is an order that must be followed. The person who's confronted the Ahab spirit must first have the legal authority to confront Ahab. What does this mean? It means that if the Ahab spirit is operating in you, you have the legal right to confront it because God made you "king" or "queen" over your own soul. However, if the person who has the Ahab spirit happens to be your pastor, you have no legal right to battle him. You can speak with him about the matter, but if he refuses to humble himself (which he likely will), you must speak with whomever is covering that church. If the leader does nothing, you need to leave that church. Sitting in the congregation claiming that God has "anointed" you to bring down your pastor is erroneous and dangerous because a servant is not authorized to rise against his master. This is why Jezebel said to Jehu, "*Is it peace, you Zimri, murderer of your master?*" To understand this question, we must understand who Zimri was.

1 Kings 16:1-4 (ESV): *And the word of the LORD came to Jehu the son of Hanani against Baasha, saying, "Since I exalted you out of the dust and made you leader over my people Israel, and you have walked in the way of Jeroboam and have made my people Israel to sin, provoking me to anger with their sins, behold, I will utterly sweep away Baasha and his house, and I will make your house like the house of Jeroboam the son of Nebat. Anyone belonging to Baasha who dies in the city the dogs shall eat, and anyone of his who dies in the field the birds of the heavens shall eat.*

1 Kings 16:8-19 (ESV): *In the twenty-sixth year of Asa king of Judah, Elah the son of Baasha began to reign over Israel in Tirzah, and he reigned two years. But his servant Zimri, commander of half his chariots, conspired against him. When he was at Tirzah, drinking himself drunk in the house of Arza, who was over the household* *in Tirzah, Zimri came in and struck him down and killed him, in the twenty-seventh year of Asa king of Judah, and reigned in his place.*

When he began to reign, as soon as he had seated himself on his throne, he struck down all the house of Baasha. He did not leave him a single male of his relatives or his friends. Thus Zimri destroyed all the house of Baasha, according to the word of the LORD, which he spoke against Baasha by Jehu the prophet, for all the sins of Baasha and the sins of Elah his son, which they sinned and which they made Israel to sin, provoking the LORD God of Israel to anger with their idols. Now the rest of the acts of Elah and all that he did, are they not written in the Book of the Chronicles of the Kings of Israel.

In the twenty-seventh year of Asa king of Judah, Zimri reigned seven days in Tirzah. Now the troops were encamped against Gibbethon, which belonged to the Philistines, and the troops who were encamped heard it said, "Zimri has conspired, and he has killed the king." Therefore all Israel made Omri, the commander of the army, king over Israel that day in the camp. So Omri went up from Gibbethon, and all Israel with him, and they besieged Tirzah. And when Zimri saw that the city was taken, he went into the citadel of the king's house and burned the king's house over him with fire and died, because of his sins that he committed, doing evil in the sight of the LORD, walking in the way of Jeroboam, and for his sin which he committed, making Israel to sin.

Like Jehu, Zimri was assigned to destroy the house of Baasha. But Zimri's sin was that he continued to walk in the ways of Jeroboam ... the very ways God judged Baasha for walking in. Nevertheless, Jezebel spoke Zimri's name because of the way Zimri died. She knew that Jehu was there to kill her, so in her last attempt at manipulation, she tried to instill fear in Jehu. First, she painted her eyes and beautified her hair. This is typical of the Jezebel personality. Jezebels will use their beauty, flattery, fear or any form of manipulation to get what they want. Nevertheless, Jehu didn't respond to Jezebel. The reason for this is ... he wasn't there to hold a conversation. He had an assignment and he was there to carry out that assignment. Instead, he spoke to Jezebel's eunuchs, asking them who was on his side. After two or three eunuchs looked at him, he told them to throw Jezebel off her wall. This is important when confronting the Jezebel spirit. If you hold a conversation with Jezebel, she will bewitch you with her words. That's why so many people go to confront Jezebel, only to find themselves coming back home holding gifts that Jezebel has given to them. I've witnessed many people fall into this trap after attempting to confront a Jezebel in their lives. They went and held a conversation with Jezebel and she managed to seduce them all over again. For example, a woman being abused by her jezebellic lover will approach her pastor in confidence and say, "I'm leaving him for good this time!" She'll stand before her pastor in confidence after her jezebellic lover has attacked her, but a few days later, that same woman can often be heard saying, "We talked." What she's saying is that she is back under his spell. She made the mistake of trying to confront Jezebel (her lover) without binding and destroying the works of Ahab (the spirit operating in her). Because of this, her jezebellic lover put on some nice clothes, got a haircut and said, "Look at your friend, Mary. Has she been happy ever since she left her husband?" This is the witchcraft spirit of Jezebel in full effect. Mary, for example, did like Zimri. She did not turn from her wicked ways and because of this, she did not find peace after leaving her husband. So the jezebellic lover will use Mary's story to convince his wife or insignificant other to stay with him.

To confront the Jezebel spirit, you first need to understand and apply the rules of engagement. You must first confront Ahab, otherwise, you are confronting the stems but not the root. Jezebel was a stem of Ahab's wicked heart. Ahab was the root of Jezebel!

CHAPTER 7

Defeating the Jezebel Spirit

Because the Jezebel spirit is common, one of the most common questions I get is: *How do I defeat Jezebel once and for all?* Truthfully, some people who pose this question are sincere and overly determined to get away from Jezebel, but at the same time, I've come across a great deal of people who don't want to be free. I've learned that some people are posing the wrong question, hoping to get the right answer. Some people's question *should* be: *Is there a way I can get the Jezebel spirit cast out of my loved ones without their permission?* And the answer to that question is a resounding *no*. A person has to want deliverance to receive it. This means that the choice is yours: if you're dealing with someone who has the Jezebel spirit and they want to keep their demon(s), you can either choose to tolerate Jezebel by tolerating them or you can walk away and make a clean cut. Of course, if you're married to someone who has the Jezebel spirit, you must stick around unless God gives you the okay to leave. However, if it's a friend or a family member (except small children), the best thing to do is walk away, sever the ungodly soul tie between you and that person and pray for them whenever possible. We can pray more effective prayers when we aren't emotionally affected by someone. Of course, you can pray in tongues and those prayers are always effective, but one thing you'll learn about God is ... He's serious about us not tolerating Jezebel. There's a reason for this, of course.

I've met countless people who've been ahab'ed by Jezebel and I can truly say that the Jezebel spirit is a powerful witchcraft spirit. I've seen how powerful Jezebel's witchcraft is over Ahab and I've watched many times as Jezebel *effortlessly* managed to re-entangle Ahab in her web of deception. I've had people to reach out to me who *genuinely* wanted to get away from Jezebel at some point, but leaving Jezebel meant taking responsibility for their own lives; this is where Jezebel managed to seduce them back into her web. Each time they returned to Jezebel after they'd managed to get away, it was obvious that her witchcraft over them had gotten stronger. How so? Most Ahabs do not like responsibility and most Ahabs were raised by someone who has the Jezebel spirit or they're married to someone who has the Jezebel spirit. Jezebel assumes the responsibilities that Ahab does not want to assume. For example, a person raised by Jezebel is oftentimes financially dependent on Jezebel, plus, Jezebel holds the key to all of their familial relationships. This means that if they want to have a relationship with their families, they must tolerate *and* impress Jezebel. Of course, in the event that the entire family is under Jezebel's witchcraft, they need to walk away from the entire family and most folks aren't willing to do that.

Ahabs tend to depend on their Jezebels for:

- **a sense of feeling loved:** Most people affected by the Ahab spirit have dealt with rejection or abuse at some point in their lives. They have been starved of love and affection and they fear losing the one person who appears to love them. Jezebels are *skilled* at making others believe that they love them when, in truth, Jezebels only love themselves.
- **a sense of feeling wanted and needed:** to ensure that their prey does not get out of the web, Jezebels tend to secure their prey with a thread of guilt. For example, a mother who has ahab'ed her son or daughter would likely pretend to be sickly or pretend that her child's defiance of her is literally killing her. Remember, Jezebels are narcissistic creatures who will stop at nothing to get what they want. This includes having the ambulance come to their houses, pick them up and

take them to the hospital when they aren't sick. A person with the Jezebel spirit will claim to not be able to breathe when defied, for example. This is to bind the defiant person in the web of guilt and to upset their family ... if the family is under her witchcraft. So, if a son told his mother that he's not going to the college she wants him to go to, she may yell, suddenly grab her chest and then, tell her daughter to call an ambulance. According to her, she's gotten dizzy and short of breath. When the family hears about her son's defiance and Jezebel manages to convince them that her *brush with death* is because of his defiance, the family Jezebels and Ahabs will all take turns lashing out at him. On top of feeling guilty, he's now being spiritually castrated and threatened by the only family he knows. Ahab then feels that his jezebellic mother needs him, plus, he has to go to the college she's picked out for him in order for her to live.

- **finances:** Honestly, most people under Jezebel's influence *(that I've personally met)* are financially dependent on Jezebel. I've witnessed a few of them trying to make a clean break away from Jezebel, only to find themselves returning to her so they can pull on her purse straps once more. When this happens, they have to go back into

Jezebel's web and Jezebel always manages to secure them with stronger cords each time. When Jezebel manages to replace JEHOVAH-JIREH (the Lord will provide) in someone's life, that person not only has to be delivered from idolatry, they will need financial counseling. If they don't get financial counseling, the hardships of life will always drive them back into Jezebel's web and with every return, Jezebel will pretty much say, "I told you so." She'll say this audibly or she'll hint around at it. After a while, the Ahab genuinely comes to believe that he or she is in need of Jezebel and running away is senseless and costly. Jezebels will also help their Ahabs get vehicles or houses they can't afford or they'll co-sign for their vehicles or homes. This ensures that the ahab'ed souls are fully or partially dependent on them, meaning, it would be much harder for them to break away from their Jezebels. If they attempt to break away, Jezebel will demand that they surrender the cars or move out of the houses they helped them get. If Jezebel's name is not on the vehicle or the house, she knows that Ahab's poor spending habits and lack of financial maturity will eventually drive him back into her web. Ahab hates confrontation, so whenever he's confronted by bill collectors, he'll run to Jezebel for safety.

- **emotional stability:** Sadly enough, most people under Jezebel's spell are emotionally unstable and the worst part is ... most of them don't realize this unless they try to get away from Jezebel. This is because the person with the Jezebel spirit usually makes them feel secure by assuming certain responsibilities in their lives. For example, a married woman whose mother has managed to ahab her may return to her mother when she has her first big fight with her husband. Instead of praying about it and talking with her husband, she will remember that her mother was always good at helping her in the area of conflict. Remember, Ahabs hate confrontation and when confronted, will almost always run to Jezebel. She may reach out to her estranged mother, reconcile with her, and tell her about her marital problems. Jezebel understands what her daughter needs from her, so she confronts her son-in-law and threatens to take her daughter away from him if he continues to do whatever it is that he's done. What has happened here is ... the daughter has placed herself back in Jezebel's tool-shed and pretty much sold herself to be Jezebel's property. She thinks that if her mother can manage to ahab her husband, things will get better in their marriage. However, this witchcraft attempt backfires because the husband suddenly realizes how much power his mother-in-law has over his wife. He then realizes that, in a sense, his wife's mother is her head or authority (husband); this is the reason she would not and could not submit or cleave to him. This only opens the door for a showdown between Jezebel and the man who's married to her Ahab. Jezebel almost always wins this war because Jezebel is married to Ahab.

- **to receive the life that they want or the life that Jezebel promised them:** Everyone is pursuing a dream, be that dream big or small. Some folks only dream of being left alone by mankind as a whole and living out their lives as hermits on secluded beaches, while others dream of living in huge houses being surrounded by lively (loud) people. To effectively bind people, Jezebel has to key-in on whatever it is that they want; that is, if what the person wants does not interfere with Jezebel's plans for them. If what that person wants does conflict with what Jezebel wants, she then has to convince them that her dreams for them are bigger and better than their own dreams. To do this, she will often promise to finance or help with *her* dreams. For example, if a man wanted to marry his high school girlfriend, but his jezebellic mother wants him to marry her best friend's daughter, the mother would reward him every time he spoke reproachfully about his girlfriend. She would even offer to pay for his wedding with the young woman that she has picked out for him. Jezebels are always working to get people to believe that they need them to not only function in life, but to attain their greatest dreams. For example, many of the Jezebels who hire or contract me to do some graphic work for them will oftentimes attempt to make me believe that my business's success is in the palms of their hands. They'll say things like, "If this goes well, Tiffany, I know a lot of people and you're going to be a very busy woman." Of course, this doesn't work with me, but it does work on many, if not most, new business owners. *This is why 80% of new businesses fail during their first year in business.* By attempting to make me feel that my success is in their hands, they are simultaneously saying that they have the power to cause my business to fail, and this isn't a fact unless I make it one. Jezebels will always zero in on your dreams or create a mental blueprint and hand it to you. They will then promise that they can give you whatever it is that you've been dreaming about *or greater* in exchange for your obedience and cooperation to their wants and demands. This is deception. The only power Jezebel has in a person's life is the power in which that person has given her.

One of the most effective cords I've seen Jezebels bind their spouses with is the desire to get back at someone who's hurt that particular spouse. A good example is a man who has been hurt by a woman in his past. He has never forgiven or gotten over that woman, but because she's gotten romantically involved with someone else, he decides to do the same. The darkness in his heart attracts Jezebel to him and his new lover senses that someone else has his heart, however, she doesn't care because she has him physically. She questions him about his past relationships and he opens up to her. She then surprises him by saying something like, "Well, don't worry about her anymore. You've got me now and I'm gonna show her how stupid she was to lose you." She has peaked his interest because she's offering to accept him while he's soul tied to another person, plus, she's offering to aid him in provoking his former lover. What she's done is:

- offered to be the other woman *mentally* as long as she isn't the other woman *physically*.
- offered to center their relationship around his former lover.

- offered to help him retaliate against his former lover.
- offered to help him make his former lover jealous.

Of course, he agrees to this arrangement and the two new lovers proceed to create more emotional and sexual soul ties. They even get married. Now that Jezebel has her Ahab, she becomes frustrated with the fact that he has a stronger soul tie with another woman than he has with her. *Jezebels tend to be very territorial and jealous.* She then uses this fact to castrate him repeatedly and to bind him in her web of guilt. She also follows up on her offer to retaliate against the former lover by reaching out to her and criticizing her for leaving him. This is Jezebel's way of saying, "Release him from your powers!" This may sound outlandish, but sadly enough, it's actually pretty common. A lot of Jezebel-Ahab relationships are centered around other people.

Staying Delivered

One of the keys to deliverance is maintaining your deliverance. Now, it may seem like we're putting the cart before the horse here, but in truth, I've found that it's better to tell people how to stay delivered before they receive deliverance than it is telling them after deliverance. The reason for this is ... some folks get so excited after they've been set free that they don't stick around or come back to get the "stay delivered" message.

Remember this: demons need a dark and filthy place to reside. This means that to maintain your deliverance, you've got to get the deliverance (cleansing) and then, you need the light (Holy Spirit). At the same time, please understand that Jezebel will try to find a new place to reside in your heart if the old chamber isn't available. For example, you may meet a Jezebel who focuses in on the fact that you're over thirty years old, unmarried and do not have children. She may use that information to usher you into a place of anxiousness or fear, which means, you will have opened up another dark place in your heart. When this happens, the Jezebel spirit will have effectively created a place for herself or for an Ahab spirit to dwell.

After she's seduced you into the darkness, she may attempt to make you feel that getting married and having children is contingent upon you remaining connected to her and doing her will. This means that she is setting herself up as a "queen" or "fertility goddess" in your life. She's attempting to usher you into full-blown idolatry.

How do you know if someone has the Jezebel spirit? Always pay attention to how they're trying to connect with you. Don't focus on a person's flattery, age, or religious title. Don't even focus on the number of followers that person has. Instead, focus on the direction in which they're attempting to go within your heart. Are they trying to instill fear in you? Are they trying to make you feel like you need them? Are they trying to connect with you using the pain you're in? Are they trying to connect with you with promises of helping you deal with some negative situation that you've found yourself in? Jezebels often catch people when they're scared, sad, anxious, co-dependent or angry. She catches them when they are experiencing heightened emotions; that way, she can establish an emotional soul tie with them and offer her help in whatever it is they are struggling with. For example, let's say that you have just heard that your child's father wants to take you to court in an attempt to gain custody of your daughter with him. He happens to be an unstable man with violent tendencies and you know that the only reason he's taking you to court is because you keep rejecting his advances. You're angry, scared, frustrated and anxious. At that moment, you are prime bait for the Jezebel spirit. Someone with the Jezebel spirit may hear about your situation and approach you. She may say, "I don't mean to pry and if I'm overstepping my boundaries, just let me know. I heard about your problems with Henry's son. I personally know Henry and if his son is anything like him, he doesn't need to be anywhere near your daughter. I just want you to know that I'm praying for you and if you need anything, please let me know. One of my good friends is a lawyer and if that doesn't work, I know a drug dealer who says that Henry owes him some money. He's been looking for Henry for a long time, so if all else fails, we'll just make sure that he finds Henry. Here's my number." What you may not realize at that moment is ... the woman standing in front of you is not offering you her friendship; she's offering you her witchcraft. Needless to say, when a woman is scared and emotionally scarred, such a woman may appear to be God-sent, but we must remember that God doesn't send bitter people to help us out of bitter situations. In this situation, you will need to regain control of your emotions, pray, fast and refuse to receive any demonic assistance. Because that's all Jezebel can offer you. In this case, what Jezebel is really saying is, "I'm a bigger and more wicked demon than the one that's in your ex. If you come under my authority, I can take jurisdiction over you and call off the attack from your ex's demons because I outrank them." If you bite this bait, you'll find yourself in a deeper pit than the one you started out in.

Staying delivered means that you may have to go through some seasons alone. You may even be required by God to move to another neighborhood, city or state.

You may have to endure persecution and go through those seasons when you have more questions than you have answers. However, if you are willing to trust God and let the Word of God ground you, you will eat the good of the land, meaning, you will inherit the victorious nature of God.

Untangling Her Web

To defeat the Jezebel spirit, you must first get out of her web. This not only requires deliverance, but it requires that you undergo a paradigm shift, meaning, your mind has to completely change. Whatever it was that allowed Jezebel in your life has to be cast out! If it was anger and frustration, you need to let it go. If it was fear and anxiety, you need to let it go. If it was lust and perversion, you need to let it go. What I've found is that deliverance comes in layers. Sometimes, we want to get delivered from the demons at the top, not realizing that it's the small foxes that are the most destructive ones. This means that you need to get delivered from the stage that Jezebel is standing on; that way, you don't get Jezebel cast out, only to find that spirit returning again and again.

Demons work in networks, and each demon has a function. People tend to have demonic habits that they need to be delivered from because some demonic spirits will establish or influence thought patterns within an individual. These thought patterns ensure that the bound person does not get free, and if they are to get set free, they will re-invite the demonic personalities back in. For example, a woman may deal with the demon responsible for the condition we now know as Obsessive Compulsive Disorder or OCD. OCD is characterized by obsessive thoughts, compulsive behaviors, and so on. She obsessively cleans her house and makes her children wash their hands every time they touch something she believes to be dirty. One day, that woman receives deliverance from one of the spirits behind OCD (fear), and all is well for about a week. However, her three-year-old daughter catches a cold and her doctor says she likely touched something that had the cold virus on it. At that moment, she can easily return to her obsessive ways and most people would. She may start making her kids scrub their hands at any given time and because she has re-opened herself for the spirit of fear, she will escalate in her behaviors. Suddenly, she's carrying around anti-bacterial soap, wipes and gels. The demon that got cast out is now being welcomed back in. That's because the deliverance minister shouldn't have focused on the OCD; he or she should have dug deeper and started casting out the stage that OCD was standing on. By digging deeper, the deliverance minister may discover that her obsessive compulsive ways are the results of some deep-rooted childhood trauma. That trauma has to be dealt with, otherwise, she'll receive deliverance on the surface, but not full deliverance because what's in the depths of her heart has not been dealt with.

Untangling Jezebel's web means that you first need to dig deeper to find out what Jezebel is standing on. Sure, anyone can say that it is the Ahab spirit that invited Jezebel into your life, and while this is true, the question remains: how did Ahab get into your life? This means you need to dig deeper. Understand this: Ahab is a king; he is a ruling spirit, which means that he *has* to have a kingdom. He needs to have some other spirits to rule. In other words, there are other spirits in operation that allowed Ahab to rise to kingship and those spirits have to be cast out as well. This also means that the Ahab spirit is not just a spirit; it is a principality. When engaging in warfare against a principality, the ruling spirit (strongman) needs to be bound and cast out.
Mark 3:27 (ESV): *But no one can enter a strong man's house and plunder his goods, unless he first binds the strong man. Then indeed he may plunder his house.*

What if the Jezebel spirit is inherited? The answer is simple; renounce the bloodline curse, dethrone the Jezebel spirit by renouncing it, and release whatever Ahabs you've taken into captivity. If you have the Jezebel spirit, you have one or more Ahabs whose authority you are walking in. Release and renounce the Ahab and the authority you have over Ahab. Sever all ungodly soul ties, forgive the folks who've hurt you, and submit yourself wholly to God. As I mentioned earlier, demons find dark patches in the heart to reside in. All too often, people will give God 90% of their hearts, thus, allowing the enemy to have access to ten percent of their hearts. This sounds like advancement, but it isn't. It only sets the stage for double-mindedness and instability. I've found that what we commonly refer to as a "storm of life" is sometimes the good in us waging war against the bad in us or vice versa. Think of it this way: how is a tornado created? The following information was taken from nationalgeographic.com regarding the formation of thunderstorms: *The most intense tornadoes emerge from what are called supercell thunderstorms. For such a storm to form, you first "need the ingredients for a regular thunderstorm," says Brooks. Those ingredients include warm moisture near the surface and relatively cold, dry air above. "The warm air will be buoyant, and like a hot-air balloon it will rise," says Brooks.*

A tornado is nothing but cold air and hot air meeting and creating an environment of instability. The same goes for us. When we are lukewarm, we cause storms to form in our lives and in the lives of others. You have to give God one hundred percent of your heart; that way, any storm that rages up against you won't be coming from within. This means you'll have the legal authority to immediately rebuke that storm and it has to obey.

One of the most important things you'll need to do is release the Ahabs in your life. This includes those friends you have who feel like they owe you something. I remember talking with a brother in Christ some years ago and he told me the story of a woman he'd once helped. The woman felt so grateful to him that she kept calling and trying to help him with any and everything he needed. He said the Lord told him that the woman felt indebted to him, so he had to put a stop to her self-imposed slavery. He couldn't receive anything from her anymore and he stopped answering her calls. He wasn't doing it to be mean; he was releasing her from the bondage she'd placed herself in. Sometimes, we have to do this with people because they do not belong to us. If someone in your life is trying to pay off some self-imposed debt or a debt that you've placed upon them, you need to release that person. If you won't release your Ahabs, Jezebel won't release you.

Matthew 18:23-35 (ESV): *Therefore is the kingdom of heaven likened unto a certain king, which would take account of his servants. And when he had begun to reckon, one was brought unto him, which owed him ten thousand* *talents. But forasmuch as he had not to pay, his lord commanded him to be sold, and his wife, and children, and all that he had, and payment to be made. The servant therefore fell down, and worshipped him, saying, Lord, have patience with me, and I will pay thee all. Then the lord of that servant was moved with compassion, and loosed him, and forgave him the debt. But the same servant went out, and found one of his fellowservants, which owed him an hundred pence: and he laid hands on him, and took him by the throat, saying, Pay me that thou owest. And his fellowservant fell down at his feet, and besought him, saying, Have patience with me, and I will pay thee all. And he would not: but went and cast him into prison, till he should pay the debt. So when his fellowservants saw what was done, they were very sorry, and came and told unto their lord all that was done. Then his lord, after that he had called him, said unto him, O thou wicked servant, I forgave thee all that debt, because thou desiredst me: Shouldest not thou also have had compassion on thy fellowservant, even as I had pity on thee? And his lord was wroth, and delivered him to the tormentors, till he should pay all that was due unto him. So likewise shall my heavenly Father do also unto you, if ye from your hearts forgive not every one his brother their trespasses.*

To untangle Jezebel's web, you need to look deep within

yourself and confront whatever hurts, confusion, and unresolved issues you find lurking. These are the cords that Jezebel is using to bind you. You need to free yourself from each one of those cords. This means that if you haven't forgiven yourself for something that has happened in your life, you need to ask the Lord to help you to forgive yourself. You have to release yourself from yourself. Sometimes, we hold ourselves in bondage. If you haven't forgiven someone, confront that issue. Ask the Lord to help you to release that person and then, open up your mouth and release them. For example, say, "I forgive John Doe for what he's done to me and I release him from any and all debt he owes to me." After that, command every spirit that came in through that unforgiveness to release you. If you know their names, call them out by name or simply say, "I renounce every unclean spirit that entered my life through unforgiveness and I bind you right now in the name of Jesus Christ. I command you to leave my heart, my soul, my body and my life and go into the abyss right now in the name of Christ Jesus." Demons cannot stay where they are not welcome and where they have no darkness to reside in. Immediately after that, ask the Holy Spirit to fill you up in the places where you've been emptied out. You must invite Him in if you don't want the demon or demons that got cast out to return. Finally, you need to maintain your deliverance by monitoring your thinking patterns. If you find yourself thinking about John Doe, cast down the thoughts and begin to pray for him. Pay attention to your friends as well. If anyone tries to usher you back into bondage, take your distance from them.

Matthew 12:43-42 (ESV): *"When the unclean spirit has gone out of a person, it passes through waterless places seeking rest, but finds none. Then it says, 'I will return to my house from which I came.' And when it comes, it finds the house empty, swept, and put in order. Then it goes and brings with it seven other spirits more evil than itself, and they enter and dwell there, and the last state of that person is worse than the first. So also will it be with this evil generation."*

Don't stop there. Keep looking for areas where you may be bound and confront those issues. You can get help with this through pastoral counseling. Don't be ashamed of your issues; confront them, and unravel yourself from them. The strength of Jezebel's web is in your self-imposed strongholds.

Reclaiming the Courts

As a reminder, the outside of the subconscious is the conscious mind and this is what's presently engaging us at any given moment. To get set free from Jezebel and other demonic entities, we must cleanse each layer of our temples.

The first layer is the outside or, better yet, the conscious mind. If we change what goes in, we can change what comes out.

Proverbs 4:23 (ISV): *Above everything else guard your heart, because from it flow the springs of life.*

We cleanse this arena of our hearts by filtering what we subject ourselves to. We learn to filter the music we listen to, what we watch on television, who we hang around and the church we become a part of.

Music: Only listen to music that agrees with the Word of God. Anything that speaks to you is supplying information to you. Every time an artist sings, that artist is releasing information that was either birthed in the artists' heart or the heart of the person they purchased the song from. The point of the song is to bring the listener into agreement with the lyrics. The goal of the bridge is to help us remember what we're saying; it's the equivalent of chanting. The goal of the beat is to make the song more entertaining and more memorable. Don't sing anything into your life or heart that a deliverance minister will eventually have to cast out of it. If the song promotes lust, premarital sex, violence, murder, pride, adultery, divorce or anything that God is against, it should not be entering your ear-gates. Understand this: music is the only source of information that does not sit in the lobby of our minds; it goes directly to the second layer of the subconscious where it is stored in our hearts and becomes one of the many wells that we source from. That's why we often say, "I know that song by heart." What we're saying is ... that song is now a part of me.

Television: Don't watch any shows or videos that promote sin. Anything that promotes sin will desensitize you to it. That's why a lot of Christians are so accepting of sins like abortion, homosexuality, premarital sex, etc. They didn't guard their ear-gates or their eye-gates and before long, they'd established a soul tie with the people they'd embraced as "celebrities." When this happens, they slowly begin to place facts where truth should be and they put the truth where we normally store facts. Many of them won't walk away from the church, but they will walk away from God. Consequentially, they will become religious and start warring against the truth and siding with the world.

Friends and family: The people we refer to as our friends and family members oftentimes have the most intimate access to us. That's why Satan loves to send people into our lives wearing friendly masks and saying whatever it is that we want to hear. That's also why he starts using our bound family members to teach us that family should never walk away from family. This ungodly truth is the reason that so many children end up molested, raped, traumatized and full of demons. The truth of the matter is ... *everyone* who has access to you intimately has access to the first and second layers of the subconscious. They can freely pour into you and challenge whatever information you have stored in you. They aren't just casual acquaintances as the devil would have you believe; they are people with passwords that allow them to go directly past the outer courts of your conscious and directly into your subconscious mind! These people directly affect what you send out and what you receive! That's why many people can testify that ever since they obeyed God and removed certain people from their lives, they immediately begin to see positive changes in their thinking, their life's results, and their finances.

Church: When we hear the word "church," most of us automatically think that we are talking about a safe place. The truth is that we are the church; *we are the temples of the Holy Spirit*. However, man commonly refers to the "building" as the church. Your "church home" is a body of people who come together for a common purpose. That collective purpose, believe it or not, was determined by the leader of that church. So, for example, if the leader is a Baal worshiper, while you happen to be Christian, you will become a Baal worshiper who identifies himself or herself as Christian. The head of that church determines the god of that church. That's why it's very important that we ask God to send us to the "church homes" that He wants us to be a part of. All too often, believers find buildings closest to their homes or start frequenting the worship assemblies that their family or friends attend, not realizing that even if they are in a godly establishment, each corporate body is at a certain level. Each level is similar to the levels in school; there are different grades and we advance to each grade by passing the previous one. Many believers are the equivalent of third graders attempting to study with twelfth graders. All the same, many believers are twelfth graders attempting to study with third graders and that's why they keep falling asleep in church. It is always better to let God lead you to where He wants you to be; that way, you can get fed what you need to grow. Additionally, if you find yourself warring; for example, with the Jezebel spirit, you will have seasoned leaders who will know how to cover you and decapitate Jezebel.

You start sweeping around the outer courts of your mind by filtering what goes in it and who has access to it. This is done by trusting God to pick your friends, your church, and your spouse. This is also done by you refusing to let any information or images that keep you from walking by the Spirit away from your ear-gates and your eye-gates. Don't let anything in you that feeds the dead nature of your flesh and compels you to sin against God. **Galatians 5:16-24 (ESV):** *But I say, walk by the Spirit, and you will not gratify the desires of the flesh. For the desires of the flesh are against the Spirit, and the desires of the Spirit are against the flesh, for these are opposed to each other, to keep you from doing the things you want to do. But if you are led by the Spirit, you are not under the law. Now the works of the flesh are evident: sexual immorality, impurity, sensuality, idolatry, sorcery, enmity, strife, jealousy, fits of anger, rivalries, dissensions, divisions, envy, drunkenness, orgies, and things like these. I warn you, as I warned you before, that those who do such things will not inherit the kingdom of God. But the fruit of the Spirit is love, joy, peace, patience, kindness, goodness, faithfulness, gentleness, self-control; against such things there is no law. And those who belong to Christ Jesus have crucified the flesh with its passions and desires.*

Next, you need to start the eviction process. Kick out any and every belief that exalts itself against the Word of God. You do this by bringing in new information and verbally rejecting the old information. This is called renunciation. Now, renunciation is not always necessary for deliverance to take place, but it does help with the process. Read your Bible, be sure to join whatever body of worshipers that God assigns you to and surround yourself with wise people.

Proverbs 13:20 (KJV): *He that walketh with wise men shall be wise: but a companion of fools shall be destroyed.*

Be sure to renounce and bind every unclean spirit that you find lurking within you. You can also employ the aid of a seasoned deliverance minister. Be sure to pray first; don't just run to the first church or person wearing a deliverance label. Some buildings may be ungodly establishments and, at the same time, some ministers aren't mature in the area of deliverance. This is why you need to pray first; that way, God will send you to a seasoned deliverance minister or He may send you to an unseasoned one and use that opportunity to train the minister. And please understand that once God begins to clean up each layer of the outer courts, it is up to you to maintain that deliverance. This means that you can't go back to doing the same things you used to do and hanging around the folks that God delivered you from. I've seen many people do this and they all ended up far more bound than they were before. They didn't value their freedom enough to maintain it.

Cleaning out the first two layers of the subconscious can be a lengthy process, depending on how much deliverance you need, how much deliverance you're able to receive at any given time, how much information you take in, how much information you retain and how determined you are to maintain your deliverance. Don't be discouraged; everyone has or had to undergo this process at some point.

The third layer of the subconscious is the part where you will likely need help if that part needs cleaning out. More than likely, if the third layer of your subconscious has been trespassed on by demons, you would not be reading this book. That's because when the third level is breached, people tend to suffer from mental health issues and severe infirmities. However, if this level has been breached in your life, you need to seek the help of a seasoned, godly deliverance minister. Pray and ask the Lord to lead you to the place where He wants you to go. He will prepare the minister for the warfare and again, you will need to replace the old information with new information. Note: This level may require fasting on your part and the part of the deliverance minister to access.

Mark 9:29 (KJV): *And he said unto them, This kind can come forth by nothing, but by prayer and fasting.*

Cleaning out the courts of your mind is necessary to receive and maintain deliverance. All too often, believers attempt to skip the "renewing of the mind" process and because of this, many believers who've received deliverance end up in demonic bondage yet again. If you have been operating under the influence of the Ahab spirit, renounce that spirit and take your authority back. Don't let Jezebel keep walking in your authority and don't be afraid of responsibility. Most people who fear responsibilities are truly afraid of failure. Don't be. Failure is a part of life; it is what helps us to appreciate the successes of life. We all fail at some point, but the wise grow wiser from their failures.

Proverbs 24:16 (ESV): *For the righteous falls seven times and rises again, but the wicked stumble in times of calamity.*

Entrance and Exit Doors

Every demonic spirit operating in your life came in through an entrance door. That door could have been generational curses or it could have been a broken relationship, whereas you never forgave the person who hurt you. Either way, to kick the enemy out of your life, you must first know how he entered your life. Some people get delivered from the Jezebel or the Ahab spirits, only to go back and pick them up again. This is because they were so focused on getting the demons out that they forgot to close the entrance doors.

I remember being at Mara's house some years ago before we started contending with one another. Roger and I had just gotten married and he was coming to the

States for about a week. He'd decided to stay at Mara's house, so I traveled to Mara's house to be with him (she lived about eight hours from me). Even though I was young in the faith, I understood what demons were and I had some informal understanding of my God-given authority.

At Mara's house, everything that could go wrong seemed to go wrong. Mara was the most controlling person I'd ever met. It was so bad that no one had to tell me that I was dealing with a demon. I'd recently gotten out of Nancy's grip, and I'd learned a little bit about the Jezebel spirit by then, so I knew without a shadow of a doubt that Mara had the Jezebel spirit. On top of that, the spirit in Mara was far more wicked and a *lot* stronger than the Jezebel that was in Nancy. This is when I learned that the Jezebel spirit in one person may be stronger and more wicked than the Jezebel in another person.

One day, a friend of mine had come to visit me at Mara's house. Mara was not home and I was in the kitchen cooking. Danielle (my friend) was standing in the kitchen's doorway talking with me. Suddenly, Danielle looked down the hallway and I remember seeing fear in her eyes. She turned her head back towards me, but she wasn't looking at me. Instead, she started staring right past me as if someone or something was standing right next to her and she was intentionally trying not to look at it. "What's wrong?" I asked. At first, Danielle didn't respond. She just kept staring right past me. A few seconds later, she slowly turned her head and looked into the hallway again. "Ummm, I don't want you to think that I'm crazy, but there's a spirit pacing up and down the hallway," she said. Amazingly enough, even though I was young in the faith, I was no longer afraid of demons. I smiled. "Well, we know what to do with him; now, don't we?" I said as I grabbed a bottle of olive oil out of the cabinet. I picked up a small coffee cup and poured a little oil in it. "Let's pray over this oil," I said. Danielle placed her hands on the cup and we begin to pray and bless the oil. After this was finished, I put my index finger in the oil and started anointing some of the doors. "In the name of Jesus, I command every demon in this house to get out now!" I shouted while looking towards the hallway. I walked into the living room and continued to command the demon to leave. By this time, Danielle was sitting on the couch and I went to sit next to her. "Where is it now?" I asked Danielle. "Still in the hallway," she responded. "And that thing is mad!" she said while staring into the hallway. I believed Danielle. I had no doubt that she'd seen a demon. Danielle was not only an evangelist, but she was a seasoned prophetess. "I don't care if it's mad," I said. Knowing that the demon was mad boosted my confidence. I knew that if it was mad, it was because our prayer and warfare were effective. "Get out of here now, devil ... in the name of Jesus Christ!" I shouted once again. That's when I felt something go past me. It didn't go out the living room door; I felt like something had walked right past Danielle and I and went out the patio doors. The patio doors were on a different wall than the front door was ... *obviously*. I didn't feel wind, nor did I feel heat. I just felt a presence passing me by. When Danielle told me that it had just left, I asked her which way it went. I wanted to test her because I was sure I felt something walk right past us. "It went out the patio doors," she said. It was at that moment that I realized that demons don't respond to human power; they respond to the name of Jesus Christ.

Later that day, Mara came home and for the first time in a few days, there was absolute peace in that house. Normally, when she came home, things would become chaotic the minute she twisted the door knob. It felt like a completely different environment, but the next day, things had returned to "abnormal." I started feeling frustrated again because everyone in the house was back to "treading softly" in an attempt to not upset Mara. Being at Mara's house meant staying out of her way as much as possible. I was praying and crying out to God because even though I was a newlywed, I knew that my marriage was not going to work with the man I'd married since he was under Mara's control.

I spent most of my time in the room praying. No one knew what I was going through but Danielle and another friend of mine and they didn't know the majority of it. For this reason, I was surprised when I received an email from an older man (he appeared to be around 70 years old). On his picture, the man was wearing a priestly collar. "I don't know who you are and I don't know anything about you, but the Lord wants me to train you for warfare," he wrote. "It's up to you. Here's my number. You can call me if you want." I grabbed my cell phone and started dialing right away.

Mr. Jones was nice but authoritative. He immediately told me how he ministered and he asked me if I wanted to proceed with training. Of course I did. I was getting my religious butt kicked by the devil. I'd had one good round where I'd kicked him out of the house, but it seemed that the tables had turned. The enemy was back and I was ready to leave.

I told Mr. Jones what I had been going through and I told him how I'd kicked the devil out of the apartment a few nights prior. He then asked me a question. "When you kicked it out, what did you do with it?" I was stumped.

What did he mean? I hadn't done anything with it. I just told it to get out. He reiterated his question. "When you kicked the devil out, where did you send it?" His voice was firm, but fatherly. I was quiet for a few seconds. "I don't know," I said. "I just told it to get out in Jesus name." Mr. Jones laughed. His laughter broke through and helped me to relax a little. I loosened up and tried to release the frustration and the fear that I had been feeling. After all, Mr. Jones was there to train me. He wasn't big on humor so hearing him laugh made me laugh. "Let me ask you a question," he said. "If I kicked you out of the house, couldn't you come back in it?" Of course, I could, but I remained quiet, worried that I'd give the wrong answer. "Yes!" he said. "If I threw you out, you could come back in easily! You have to tell it where to go, baby girl. That's why they came back! You have pissed them off and that's why they're fighting you so hard!"

I continued talking with Mr. Jones for several months, learning more and more about demonic spirits. *What's the point?* I recognized that there was an exit door and I kicked a demon out of it, but I didn't realize that there was an entrance door. I didn't realize that the same demon I'd kicked out could come back in. Mr. Jones didn't teach me how to perform deliverance on myself or anyone else. Instead, he taught me how demons reason and he told me a lot of stories about deliverances he'd performed. I now realize that God sent him to open my understanding in regards to the spirit realm.

Another brother of Christ of mine said something to me that helped me to further understand demonic jurisdiction. He said, "You can't kick the devil out of his own house. That was her [Mara's] house and she'd welcome those spirits in her house and in her life." He went on to tell me that you don't go to a witch's house and try to cast the devil out of it. Doing so only invites unnecessary warfare. The same is true in deliverance. You can't set someone free who doesn't want to be free.

Entrance and exit doors work this way. Demons come in through a door and that door has oftentimes been opened by sin, generational curses, ungodly soul ties, ungodly oaths and so on. People don't necessarily have to repent of the sin that let the devil in to be delivered from the demons, but they do need to repent to remain free. If not, they'll only return to the sin and re-invite the devil back into their lives.
Proverbs 36:11 (ESV): *Like a dog that returns to his vomit is a fool who repeats his folly.*

To be delivered from generational curses, you need to renounce those generational and bloodline curses. Additionally, you can't walk in the same manner or direction that your family once walked in. You have to take a different path and sometimes, this means that you have to walk away from the people that you are most familiar with and that's family. As for sins, you have to:

- **renounce the sins:** You don't have to renounce all of your sins audibly; after all, sometimes, we commit sins that we aren't aware of, but it is good to verbally renounce the ones you are aware of. In Psalm 19:12 (NIV), David said, "But who can discern their own errors? Forgive my hidden faults."
- **repent of the sins:** one of the most important parts of deliverance is repentance. The reason for this is ... sin represents a dark place. Each dark place in your heart gives place to the devil (Ephesians 4:27). Casting the devil out of the darkness does not remove the darkness. You need to turn the lights on by repenting of those sins, which means that you have to acknowledge that you were wrong and turn back to Christ Jesus. Sometimes, we are turned to Christ with our mouths, but our hearts are turned away from Him. Repentance means turning back around; it is embracing a paradigm shift, whereas, you are committing to walk in the ways of Christ and not in your former ways.

- **bind and cast out the spirits:** You do this by audibly speaking to them and telling them to leave. For example, when I rejected the spirit of rejection, I said to it, "Spirit of rejection, I want nothing to do with you. I renounce you and I bind you in the name of Jesus Christ. I command you to come out of me and go into the abyss in the name of Christ Jesus. Go now!" Not long after uttering those words, I found myself standing over the toilet and spitting up. This is common in deliverance. I also spit out the Ahab spirit. I believe I got delivered from the Jezebel spirit years earlier when the Lord had me doing things that were foreign to me. He'd told me to submit to Roger and He'd started telling me how to speak and treat him. I obeyed Him and a lot of things changed in my life for the better, including my mind. In other words, not all demons have to be called out; some of them come out when you stop feeding them.
- **ask the Holy Spirit to fill you where you've been emptied out:** The Holy Spirit represents the light of God. Wherever there was darkness in your life, you need Him to enter that place to breathe life into it. Remember, sin causes us to "sear" or "wither up" our minds in certain areas and it is those dead, dry places that demons

move into. Once you've gone through deliverance, those areas become what can best be described as "spiritual ghost towns." When you ask the Holy Spirit to fill you up, you're asking Him to move into that place and liven it up.

- **maintain your deliverance:** One of the biggest problems I've witnessed is folks going through deliverance, only to go back to their former ways. One of the reasons for this is ... some people don't want to give up the sin; they just want the consequences to be kicked out. Weeks or months later, they are in need of more deliverance because they keep hanging around the very people God told them to get away from and they keep doing the very things that God told them to stop doing. If you want deliverance, you have to be willing to make some sacrifices to stay delivered. Deliverance isn't a one-time event. I've had to go through several deliverances and this is what compelled me to start paying attention to my life, choices, thinking patterns, and connections. I remember going through my second deliverance and wondering why I needed more deliverance. I thought after kicking the devil out, I'd be okay, but it took more than that. I needed a new mind and once I received a renewed mind, I needed to stop letting old wineskins (friends) attempt to pour into me. Deliverance has to be a lifestyle; it is *not* a one time event.

Demons often exit through our breathing passages (mouth and nose) because they are spirits and spirits are like air. Remember, Satan is the prince of the power *of the* air. When going through deliverance, you'll likely notice yourself yawning, coughing, breathing heavily, burping, coughing up phlegm, blowing your nose, sneezing or vomiting. These are all normal responses to deliverance so don't be surprised. Make sure you're near a toilet or you have some paper towels handy. Sometimes, paper towels aren't enough so make sure that you at least have a small trash can handy. You can take yourself through deliverance (like I did) or you can let someone else take you through deliverance. It's your choice, but I recommend that you be led by the Holy Spirit.

Push Jezebel Off Her Wall

After you've received deliverance from the Jezebel or the Ahab spirit (or both), you need to learn to guard yourself against those spirits. Think of it this way. If you were a high school student and you had a bully who took a class with you, kicking him out that class wouldn't stop him from bullying you. It would only stop him from bullying you in *that* classroom. However, whenever and wherever he finds you, he will confront and attack you. Bullies are attracted to fear and we all know that the most effective way to stop a bully is to confront him or her. The same goes for the Jezebel spirit. Kicking Jezebel out of your temple won't stop her from pursuing you. It'll only stop her from attacking you from *within*. That spirit will still attack you by sending demonically bound people into your life (whenever possible), or by using people to attack you in the workplace, family, church or wherever they have access to you. You don't fight Jezebel by avoiding her; you fight her by confronting her and pushing her off her wall. Jezebel's wall represents the window of the temple in which she resides. This is a picture of deliverance. The castle was the building in which Jezebel lived. When the eunuchs pushed her off her wall, they basically threw her out the window.

2 Kings 9:30-33 (ESV): *When Jehu came to Jezreel, Jezebel heard of it. And she painted her eyes and adorned her head and looked out of the window. And as Jehu entered the gate, she said, "Is it peace, you Zimri, murderer of your master?" And he lifted up his face to the window and said, "Who is on my side? Who?" Two or three eunuchs looked out at him. He said, "Throw her down." So they threw her down. And some of her blood spattered on the wall and on the horses, and they trampled on her.*

Warfare is most effective when it's done in numbers and

in unity. Talk with your church's leaders and let them know what's going on in your life. Let them know that you're having a lot of problems with the Jezebel spirit pursuing you. If they are your God-assigned leaders, they will know how to pray for you; if not, God may give them a strategy. Come together with your leaders or your siblings in Christ and begin to pray against Jezebel. You have to open your mouth. Complaining about Jezebel won't make that spirit leave you alone; you are a vessel of power. Open your mouth and release the power of God. When you come together with your sisters and brothers in the Lord, all of you are joining together as one against that spirit. You become conduits of power, releasing a strong attack against Jezebel in the realm of the spirit.

Matthew 18:20 (ESV): *For where two or three are gathered together in my name, there am I in the midst of them.*

Ecclesiastes 4:12 (KJV/2000): *And if one prevails against him, two shall withstand him; and a threefold cord is not quickly broken.*

Always remember that the power is in your mouth. I had to stop complaining about Jezebel and I had to stop hiding from her. When I stopped hiding and I began to walk in the authority that God had given me, He blessed me to start operating in the ministry of deliverance.

Nowadays, my conference calls draw hundreds of people from around the world who are seeking deliverance and God has been on every last one of those calls to set the captives free. I realize now that Jezebel's job was to muzzle me and make me afraid of my own God-given authority. However, when I started fighting back, I discovered a power that was within me that the enemy could not touch and now I know why Jezebel was after me.

In Marriage: If you happen to be married to someone with the Jezebel spirit, you will need to intercede for your spouse. If you're the wife of someone who has the Jezebel spirit, remember Queen Esther. She won over a pagan king by simply surrounding herself with counselors, being open to listen to those counselors and by submitting to her king. Submission is a powerful weapon against the enemy and that's why he'll tempt you to fight back, instead of submitting. Submission brings you into unity with your husband and Satan is powerless in unity. If you are a man who's married to a woman with the Jezebel spirit, you need to pray, ask God to build your confidence, and take your authority back. You cannot overcome Jezebel without your authority. Jezebellic wives tend to threaten to leave their husbands and take their children from them. If your wife does this, tell her that she is free to leave. You should *never* submit to Jezebel. By standing your ground, what you're doing is forcing her to choose between submitting to her demons or submitting to you. If you need to leave (temporarily) to keep the peace, do so. When she's calm and ready to talk, suggest Christian counseling. Take her to a deliverance ministry so she can come to understand what the Jezebel spirit is, but again, make sure you pray before you choose a church.

Sadly enough, not all spouses will turn away from their wicked ways. I've learned that a lot of people actually love having demonic personalities and any deliverance minister will tell you that if you attempt to deliver someone who doesn't want to be delivered, their demons will speak out and say things like, "I'm not coming out" or "You can't make me come out." In some cases, of course, the demons are lying and attempting to dissuade the minister, but in some cases, the minister will bring the person back to a conscious state and tell them to release whatever or whomever it is that they need to release. Sometimes, folks simply refuse to release the folks who've hurt them, and when this happens, the person has to go home with their demons ... even though the minister may bind them up. Binding them simply renders them powerless.

If your spouse refuses to get delivered, you will have to

be a light in your own home. Remain prayerful and even when you're tempted to respond in an ungodly way ... don't! Demons feed on division, pride, anger, wrath and any form of sin that's available for them to feed on. You will need to utilize this time to practice humbling yourself in the midst of chaos. Eventually, your spouse will either choose to come to Christ and get delivered or that spouse may choose to leave you altogether. That's because darkness and light cannot dwell together and if the person simply does not want deliverance, even after seeing you operating as a light in the home, God won't force that person to get delivered. Should the spouse choose to leave, the Bible tells us to let the unbeliever go.
1 Corinthians 7:15 (ESV): *But if the unbelieving partner separates, let it be so. In such cases the brother or sister is not enslaved. God has called you to peace.*

Needless to say, remain positive. Who knows which direction your marriage will go but God?
1 Corinthians 7:16 (ESV): *For how do you know, wife, whether you will save your husband? Or how do you know, husband, whether you will save your wife?*

Family and Friends: You have to sever soul ties and associations with any and everyone who does not want to be set free. Sometimes, a deliverance minister does not want to tell you this, but it is true. Of course, the right thing to do is talk to your friends and family members and try to get them to come to church with you. Because of familiarity, they may not be able to hear from you, so they may need to hear from someone else. Be a light in their midst and invite them to church. Talk to them about Christ and talk to them about their ways. Make sure that you are led by the Spirit of God in your conversations with them. If they do not want to be set free, you have to cut ties with them. Understand this: they have access to the intimate portions of your soul and they will pour things into your life that you will ultimately have to get cast out of it.

Church: If your leader has the Jezebel spirit, you need to leave that church. Ask God to send you wherever He wants you to go. I've seen far too many cases of believers who've sat under questionable leadership, claiming that they were "anointed" to be there. Then, they'd ask for prayers because of the many attacks they were enduring. What they didn't realize was ... God didn't "anoint" them to sit under Jezebel. They were simply too afraid and too comfortable to leave and by staying, they ended up in rebellion.

2 Corinthians 6:17-18 (ESV): *Therefore go out from their midst, and be separate from them, says the Lord, and touch no unclean thing; then I will welcome you, and*

I will be a father to you, and you shall be sons and daughters to me, says the Lord Almighty."

Lastly, if you happen to be the person who has the Jezebel spirit, please understand that you and Jezebel are not one; you are a separate personality who's been invaded by another personality. God can and will deliver you *if you want deliverance*. Don't see yourself as the villain; see yourself as a person who's been granted the opportunity to push Jezebel off her wall yet again. Once you're free from the Jezebel spirit, God may use you to expose and cast out the Jezebel spirit that's operating in the lives of others. Don't try to cast Jezebel out of someone else's life when Jezebel or Ahab is clearly operating in your life.
Matthew 7:3-5 (ESV): *Why do you see the speck that is in your brother's eye, but do not notice the log that is in your own eye? Or how can you say to your brother, 'Let me take the speck out of your eye,' when there is the log in your own eye? You hypocrite, first take the log out of your own eye, and then you will see clearly to take the speck out of your brother's eye.*

Remember, you are the temple of the Holy Spirit. You can't ask the devil to leave; you have to tell him to leave. You have to drive him out. A great example of what deliverance looks like is found in the story of Jesus driving the money-changers out of the temple.

Matthew 21:12-15 (NLT): *Jesus entered the Temple and began to drive out all the people buying and selling animals for sacrifice. He knocked over the tables of the money changers and the chairs of those selling doves. He said to them, "The Scriptures declare, 'My Temple will be called a house of prayer,' but you have turned it into a den of thieves!"*

The blind and the lame came to him in the Temple, and he healed them. The leading priests and the teachers of religious law saw these wonderful miracles and heard even the children in the Temple shouting, "Praise God for the Son of David."

This was a beautiful picture of deliverance. Jesus cast the thieves out of the temple before He proceeded to heal and deliver others. He didn't try to reason with the thieves; He didn't even ask them why they were there. He simply drove them out. John's account of the event was more detailed.

John 2:13-17 (ESV): *The Passover of the Jews was at hand, and Jesus went up to Jerusalem. In the temple he found those who were selling oxen and sheep and pigeons, and the money-changers sitting there. And making a whip of cords, he drove them all out of the temple, with the sheep and oxen. And he poured out the coins of the money-changers and overturned their tables. And he told* *those who sold the pigeons, "Take these things away; do not make my Father's house a house of trade." His disciples remembered that it was written, "Zeal for your house will consume me."*

Remember, the Passover was a celebration of deliverance in itself. It was the celebration of when the descendants of Abraham, Isaac and Jacob had been delivered from Egypt, and it commemorated the day when the Lord struck down every firstborn man and animal in Egypt. The Passover is a reminder of God's grace and how God passed over the homes of His beloved people. God gave them a set of instructions and one of those instructions was to take the blood of a blemish-free lamb and place it over their doorposts. After that, they were to eat the lamb with unleavened bread.

Exodus 12:7-13 (NIV): *Then they are to take some of the blood and put it on the sides and tops of the doorframes of the houses where they eat the lambs. That same night they are to eat the meat roasted over the fire, along with bitter herbs, and bread made without yeast. Do not eat the meat raw or boiled in water, but roast it over a fire—with the head, legs and internal organs. Do not leave any of it till morning; if some is left till morning, you must burn it. This is how you are to eat it: with your cloak tucked into your belt, your sandals on your feet and your staff in your hand. Eat it in haste; it is the LORD's*

Passover.
"On that same night I will pass through Egypt and strike down every firstborn of both people and animals, and I will bring judgment on all the gods of Egypt. I am the Lord. *The blood will be a sign for you on the houses where you are, and when I see the blood, I will pass over you. No destructive plague will touch you when I strike Egypt.*

This is a representation of true deliverance. Here's what we should take from this:

1. Jesus drove the thieves out of the Temple. We are the temples of the Holy Spirit and the Bible calls Satan a *liar* and a *thief.*
2. The thieves did not resist the Lord because they couldn't. Demons still can't resist the name of Jesus. They have to leave when He shows up.
3. Jesus *violently* cast the thieves out of the Temple. We have to do the same with demonic spirits. Most of them won't leave without putting up a fight. You are the temple of the Holy Spirit and as such, you are a representation of the Kingdom of God. The Kingdom of Heaven suffered violence and the violent take it by force. The question is: who's more violent: you or the demons in your life?
4. Jesus didn't just cast the thieves out; He also told the people who were selling pigeons to take the

items they were selling away. All too often, people go through deliverance but want to hold on to the benefits the devil promised them. For example, let's consider a woman who's engaged in subtle prostitution, whereas, she dates and has sex with men because she wants them to take care of her. If that woman got saved and delivered, she would still need to give up the gifts she received from those men. If she did not, she would have the thieves cast out of her, but not their stuff. Eventually, they'd return because their "booths" and their merchandise were still available in her heart.

5. We have to be zealous for the things of God. The Disciples remembered that it was written of the Christ, *"Zeal for your house will consume me."* Your body is the Temple of the Holy Spirit. You have to be zealous or committed to getting free and staying freed.
6. During the Passover, the Jews had to place the blood of a blemish-free lamb over their doorposts. Of course, we know that Jesus is the Lamb of God and He was and is without sin (blemish). His blood has to cover the doorposts of our hearts; this is what shuts off access to the enemy. Egyptians weren't allowed in the homes of the Jews. What does this mean? Don't let anything

foreign in your heart. The doorpost represents the entrance to your heart. These entrances include: your ear-gates, eye-gates and associations. Don't allow foul things in your life, otherwise, you will have allowed a foreigner in your home. Jezebel was a foreigner who should have never stepped foot in Israel. Nevertheless, when her feet touched the soil of Israel, her foreign gods (demons) came with her. Jezebel didn't come alone; she brought an entire principality (demonic kingdom) with her. The same goes for the Jezebel spirit. If you allow it in your heart, it will bring a network of demonic spirits with it.

7. The Jews had to eat the lamb with unleavened bread. Unleavened bread was bread without any rising agents like yeast. A little leaven was enough to permeate an entire lump of bread. Leaven is symbolic of sin. Galatians 5:9 (ESV) reads, *"A little leaven leavens the whole lump."* What God is saying is a little (tolerated) sin can permeate an entire nation. Any little sin you refuse to repent of is enough to hinder your full deliverance or to open you back up for demonic infestation. You can't tolerate sin at all. Sure, we won't be perfect, but if we stumble, we know to get back up, repent, and try again. If you continue in sin, sin will continue in you, and you will even-

tually give place to the devil.

8. The Lord also said, "*This is how you are to eat it: with your cloak tucked into your belt, your sandals on your feet and your staff in your hand. Eat it in haste; it is the* L*ORD's Passover.*" This is a representation of the armor of God. The blood of the lamb posted over the door represented the helmet of salvation. Every house that had the blood of a lamb on its doorpost was saved from God's judgment. The cloak to be worn was symbolic of the breastplate of righteousness. The cloak was to be tucked into the belt. The belt was a representation of the belt of truth. The sandals to be worn represented "feet prepared with the gospel of peace." The staff represented the sword of the Spirit and, of course, the shield of faith could not be seen. Faith is evident in our works, therefore, their obedience was their shields of faith. You need to put on the whole armor of God, meaning, you can't return to Egypt (the bondage of sin), otherwise, you'll have to deal with Pharaoh and his guards (Satan and his demons). Remember, when the Jews asked for time off to worship God, Pharaoh made their workload unbearable. The same goes with demonic spirits. If you get delivered and let them back in, they will make your bondage unbearable to ensure that you don't get

delivered again.

God said that when He sees the blood, He will pass over His people, meaning, He won't bring judgment upon us. He will and has extended grace to us. Don't take grace for granted and don't let the Lord's crucifixion be in vain in your life. The blood of Jesus is available to you. Use it. Let God set you free. Remember, Jezebel cannot operate where she has no authority. Take your authority back and learn to walk in it!

CHAPTER 8

Attacking the Root

Everything that exists has a root or a beginning and everything that grows only grows because it is in its ideal climate. For example, Florida provides the ideal climate for palm trees, but most palm trees cannot withstand the harsh winters of New York. For this reason, northern states are not ideal for growing palm trees. What does this mean for us? Anytime a seed is sown into us, that seed's survival is dependent on the condition of our hearts.

To take down Jezebel, you have to let God give you a new heart and a new mind, plus, you have to uproot Jezebel's seeds in your life. But before we talk about Jezebel's roots in your life, let's discuss Jezebel's roots altogether.

"Sidon, called Saida today (Arabic for "fishing"), was named after the firstborn son of Canaan (Genesis 10:15) and probably settled by his descendants. The northern border of ancient Canaan extended to Sidon (Genesis 10:19). Later, Jacob spoke of it as the boundary of Zebu lun (Genesis 49:13) and Joshua included it as part of the land promised to Israel (Joshua 13:6). Sidon was included in the inheritance of Asher, on its northern boundary (Joshua 19:28), but it was not taken by that tribe in conquest (Judges 1:31, 3:3). Settled from the beginning as a port city, Sidon was built on a promontory with a nearby offshore island that sheltered the harbor from storms." (Reference: biblearchaeology.org)

Jezebel was from the city of Sidon which, of course, was a city in ancient Phoenicia. Sidonians are believed to be Canaanites. As a matter of fact, Phoenicians spoke the Canaanite language. Why is this important? This is to help us to go back to the roots of the woman, Jezebel.

The Canaanites were named after Noah's grandson, Canaan. They were the descendants of Canaan. Sidon, the city in which Jezebel hailed from, was named after Canaan's son, Sidon. Canaan was cursed by Noah and therefore, his descendants were accursed.

Genesis 9:18-27 (ESV): *The sons of Noah who went forth from the ark were Shem, Ham, and Japheth. (Ham was the father of Canaan.) These three were the sons of Noah, and from these the people of the whole earth were dispersed.*

Noah began to be a man of the soil, and he planted a vineyard. He drank of the wine and became drunk and lay uncovered in his tent. And Ham, the father of Canaan, saw the nakedness of his father and told his two brothers outside. Then Shem and Japheth took a garment, laid it on both their shoulders, and walked backward and covered the nakedness of their father. Their faces were turned backward, and they did not see their father's nakedness. When Noah awoke from his wine and knew what his youngest son had done to him, he said, "Cursed be Canaan; a servant of servants shall he be to his brothers." He also said, "Blessed be the Lord, the God of Shem; and let Canaan be his servant. May God enlarge Japheth, and let him dwell in the tents of Shem, and let Canaan be his servant."

Why did Noah curse Canaan? The Bible tells us that Ham "uncovered his father's nakedness." Now, historians have tried to determine the meaning of "uncovering his father's nakedness." Some historians believe it to mean that Ham had homosexual relations with his drunken father. Other historians believe it to mean that Ham castrated his father which, of course, is erroneous given the fact that when Noah woke up, he cursed Ham and blessed his other two sons. The Bible never said he was wounded in any way and I think we can all agree that if his testicles had been cut off, he would not have slept through the castration, nor would he have sat there and blessed his other two sons. He would have cursed Ham for sure, but he would have been more concerned about his wound than releasing a blessing to his other sons. Another theory is that Ham had sex with his mother. This belief is fueled by Deuteronomy 22:30, which reads, "A man shall not take his father's wife, so that he does not uncover his father's nakedness" and Deuteronomy 27:20 (ESV), which reads, "Cursed be anyone who lies with his father's wife, because he has uncovered his father's nakedness.' And all the people shall say, 'Amen.'" Another scriptural reference supporting this theory is Leviticus 18:6-8 (ESV), which reads, "None of you shall approach any one of his close relatives to uncover nakedness. I am the Lord. You shall not uncover the nakedness of your father, which is the nakedness of your mother; she is your mother, you shall not uncover her nakedness. You shall not uncover the nakedness of your father's wife; it is your father's nakedness."

Needless to say, most believers simply believe that Ham "exposed" his father, instead of covering him, whereas, Shem and Japheth were intentional about covering their father and not looking at him. During that time, it was very important that children maintained respect for their father. Don Stewart writes: *"In the ancient world merely seeing one's father naked was a highly offensive act. The father's position as moral and spiritual head would be held in disrepute and the family unit would suf-*

fer as a result of this. The culture in which this event occurred considered it a capital crime for a child to strike their father." (Reference: blueletterbible.org/ Don Stewart: Why Was Canaan Cursed Instead of Ham?)

When Ham uncovered his father, he was inciting rebellion. He was not honoring his father; instead, he utilized his father's drunkenness as an opportunity to do evil to him, whether that evil was sleeping with his mother or simply exposing his father to his brothers. By uncovering his father's nakedness, Ham was inciting rebellion by attempting to "expose" his father. This is similar to what Absalom did when he had sex with David's concubines in plain view of all of Israel (2 Samuel 16:22). Absalom was declaring his father dead by having sex with his concubines. He was setting himself up to take his father's position.

When Ham uncovered his father, he was exposing his father in a moment of weakness. This was blatant disrespect and a sign of dishonor. Exposing others is the way of the Jezebel spirit. Jezebels love to incite rebellion by threatening or attempting to expose others. This is one of her trademarks.

Jezebel was more than likely a Canaanite, and as such, she carried the curse of Canaan on her. The Canaanites were polytheistic, meaning, they worshiped many gods, with Baal being their supreme god. Something we should note is that anytime God removed His blessing from a person or a group of people, He was essentially removing Himself from them. Some of the curses could include:

- the ground being cursed and mankind having to toil the ground to yield a harvest.
- the ground being cursed for a period of time, and therefore, being unable to bear fruit.
- extensive droughts.
- barren wombs.
- ... and the worst of them all, a reprobate mind.

To have a reprobate mind means to be rejected by God altogether. It means that God will turn you over to the enemy in which you serve. The Greek word for "reprobate" is "adokimos," which, according to Strong's Concordance, means: failing to pass the test, unapproved, counterfeit. Strong's Exhaustive Concordance translates the word "adokimos" as: castaway, rejected, reprobate. Having a reprobate mind means that God has removed Himself from the person He's turned over to the reprobate mind. This means that the third level or unconscious mind of the person in question is no longer off limits to demons. It means that God has essentially divorced the person. When a person has a reprobate mind, that person will openly and willingly blaspheme the Holy Spirit and sin against God without remorse. Such a soul will be overcome with hatred, overridden by demons, and overindulgent in regards to lust. He or she will have no love and no concept of right or wrong. Such a person can be fully possessed by demons and will be nothing more than a walking demon himself or herself. A person with a reprobate mind is a person whom Jesus has "spit out" or "cast out" of His body. Remember, we are all *members* of the "body" of Christ and as such, we must remain in agreement with the Lord. If we do not, Jesus will perform self-deliverance and cast us out of His body. In deliverance, people often "spit" or vomit. Jesus is saying here that He will do the same thing, but He won't be spitting out demons, since demon spirits cannot dwell in Him. Instead, He'll be casting out double-minded people who can't seem to decide whether they want to serve Him or serve their demons. He's casting out people who love darkness because darkness cannot dwell in Him. Remember: He is light and light has no communion (association) with darkness! Communion comes from the word "common" and it means: likeness, intimacy, fellowship. It is also associated with the word "communication," meaning, the Lord has nothing left to say to the enemy other than His already declared Word.

Revelation 3:16 (ESV): *So, because you are lukewarm,*

and neither hot nor cold, I will spit you out of my mouth.

The Canaanites were castaways; they had been rejected by God, and therefore, they worshiped other deities. They indeed had reprobate minds. A castaway was someone God had cast out of His presence. He cast Adam and Eve out of the Garden of Eden. This is because the Garden of Eden was blessed and Adam and Eve brought a curse upon themselves when they sinned against God. Because they were no longer blessed, they could not dwell in a holy place.

Leviticus 18:24-28 (ESV): *Do not make yourselves unclean by any of these things, for by all these the nations I am driving out before you have become unclean, and the land became unclean, so that I punished its iniquity, and the land vomited out its inhabitants. But you shall keep my statutes and my rules and do none of these abominations, either the native or the stranger who sojourns among you (for the people of the land, who were before you, did all of these abominations, so that the land became unclean), lest the land vomit you out when you make it unclean, as it vomited out the nation that was before you.*

God drove many pagan nations out of the lands they dwelt in and gave their land to the Israelites. This is a picture of deliverance taking place. God allows holy people to stay in blessed places, but anytime a person or a group of people begin to rebel against God, He will eventually cast them out of His blessings. All the same, when God places His blessing on a person or a group of people, He will cast them out of any land or from amongst any people that He has removed Himself from. For example, God delivered the Israelites from Egypt. This is another picture of deliverance, but instead of casting the ungodly out of a godly land, God was delivering the godly people from an ungodly land. God will deliver His people from demonic spirits, but all the same, He will deliver His people from people who have demonic spirits.

Ham's heart was wicked and that's why Noah cursed his seed (the unborn generations). Noah had to distinguish his seed from his brothers' seed because it was clear that Ham's heart was against his father and not for him. This is similar to what a farmer does. A farmer must identify the seeds he's growing; that way, he won't plant different seed types in one garden because some seeds can grow up and choke the others. Each seed type needs its own unique place to grow. By calling Shem and Japheth blessed and cursing the seed of Ham, Noah was making a distinction between good and evil. He was separating the wheat from the tares. This distinction was necessary to contain evil as much as possible and ensure that it would not spread amongst God's people. Noah's decree wasn't designed to hurt or embarrass Ham. It was designed to keep Ham and his children from infecting Shem, Japheth and their children. It was also a way of casting out Ham's seed, all of which, shared their father's blood and would therefore, grow up to be just like him. This was another picture of deliverance. Noah's sons were his seeds and they'd all grown up, but just like any garden, Noah had to prune the bad away from the good. He had to separate the wheat from the tares. One of the lessons to be learned from this is ... just like we have to watch out for jezebellic leaders, leaders have to watch out for jezebellic sons and daughters! Why is this? Just like Ham, a jezebellic son or daughter will uncover their leader if given the opportunity. This is why Jezebels are always trying to establish soul ties with leaders. If a leader opens his or her life to a person who has the Jezebel spirit, that person will try to learn as much about that leader as possible. This is called sequestering information. Jezebels want to know a leader's secrets, weaknesses, strengths and anything they believe they can use to either control a leader or expose that leader. They will then expose the leader's nakedness or, better yet, the leader's imperfections.

1 Peter 4:8 (ESV): *Above all, keep loving one another earnestly, since love covers a multitude of sins.*

Now, this does not mean that members should ignore their leaders' transgressions, but what it does mean is that members should intercede for their leaders, instead of exposing them. They should cover their leaders, meaning, they stand in the gap for them and keep the birds of prey (Jezebels) from devouring them. Additionally, the elders should come together and correct the leader if the leader is in error.

Galatians 6:1 (ESV): *Brothers, if anyone is caught in any transgression, you who are spiritual should restore him in a spirit of gentleness. Keep watch on yourself, lest you too be tempted.*

If the leader refuses to repent, the members should disconnect themselves from that body and let God choose for them another leader. This means that they should look for another church home!

Matthew 5:30 (ESV): *And if your right hand causes you to sin, cut it off and throw it away. For it is better that you lose one of your members than that your whole body go into hell.*

Psalm 1:1-2 (ESV): *Blessed is the man who walks not in the counsel of the wicked, nor stands in the way of sinners, nor sits in the seat of scoffers; but his delight is in the law of the Lord, and on his law he meditates day and night.*

Can you have a spiritual father or mother who has the Jezebel spirit and still remain blessed? Consider this. When Ahab sinned against God and would not fully repent, God sent Jehu to destroy his bloodline. He was cleansing the land of Ahab and Jezebel's wicked lineage. If you are submitted to a wicked leader, you will inherit the curse of that leader because you are operating as that leader's son or daughter. This is why it is important that you always ask the Lord to send you to the church that He wants you to be a part of. All too often, people sit at Jezebel's table (ministry) and claim that they are "anointed" to be there. God did not anoint you to be poisoned by anyone. If Jezebel is your spiritual mother, you will inherit the judgment of Jezebel, just as the Canaanites were cursed because of Ham.

You have to destroy Jezebel at the roots! Think of it this way: Jezebel was never supposed to step one foot into Israel, let alone rule over God's people. Israel was a body that was submitted to God, with each person being a member of that body. Ahab was the head of that body. He was supposed to lead Israel by following God. As the head of Israel, Ahab simultaneously determined the "state" of the people or, better yet, their condition. When choosing a wife, Ahab should have considered the people God had entrusted him to lead. Proverbs 12:4 says, "An excellent wife is the crown of her husband, but she

who brings shame is like rottenness in his bones." Instead of choosing a wife who could be a crown to himself, Ahab chose a wife whose bitterness and ungodly ways would be a snare to him and most of Israel. The only people who were spared from Jezebel's poisonous doctrines were the ones who separated themselves and refused to bow to Baal.
1 Kings 19:18 (ESV): "*Yet I will leave seven thousand in Israel, all the knees that have not bowed to Baal, and every mouth that has not kissed him.*"

To rid Israel of Jezebel's witchcraft and evil ways, God sent Jehu to destroy Jezebel and Ahab's bloodline. This means that He was casting Jezebel out of His people. We have to do the same. Like the Canaanites, the Jezebel root could be a generational curse in your family. How do you lift the curse? Through salvation, deliverance and by embracing a renewed mind. You need to renounce the bloodline curse and then, bind up and cast out the spirits that came in through the curse. Please remember that if the bloodline is cursed, it will remain cursed, but you can cancel it out of your blood by overriding it with the blood of Jesus Christ. Each individual adult in your family will have to do the same. You can say, for example: "I repent of my sins and the sins of my ancestors. In the name of Christ Jesus, I renounce every ungodly oath, bloodline curse and iniquity that was passed down to me from my parents, grandparents and ancestors on both sides of my family. I renounce and break every ungodly soul tie that was established in my life through my own doings and through the actions of my parents, grandparents and ancestors. I take authority over every unclean spirit that has entered my life through those generational curses, oaths and soul ties and I command those spirits to leave me now and go into the abyss in the name of Christ Jesus. I loose myself and future generations from the curses and oaths passed down from me or my ancestors to them in the name of Christ Jesus. I command every unclean spirit that entered my children, grandchildren and great grandchildren to loose them now and go into the abyss in the name of Christ Jesus."

Dealing with the root also means dealing with the fruit. One of the biggest mistakes believers make after deliverance is ... they keep operating in the fruit of demons and those fruit eventually open them back up for demonic infestation. This means that if you are delivered from the Jezebel spirit, you shouldn't keep trying to control or manipulate people. If you are delivered from the Ahab spirit, you shouldn't keep letting folks control, manipulate and dominate you. Walk in your God-given authority. When you do this, you will lose your fear of responsibility, failure, and change. This is why we have to embrace a new heart and a new mind, otherwise, we'll try to go about doing things the old way.

Matthew 9:17 (ESV): *Neither is new wine put into old wineskins. If it is, the skins burst and the wine is spilled and the skins are destroyed. But new wine is put into fresh wineskins, and so both are preserved.*

Let the condition of your new heart be one that Jezebel's seeds cannot grow or flourish in. You do this by not returning to your old ways or allowing people to contaminate you with their ungodly mindsets. Let the condition of your heart be one that attracts the blessings of God. Don't be afraid to offend people. That was a fear that I had to get past, but when I did, my peace was restored, my business's revenue more than quadrupled and God started opening new doors for me. Sure, no one likes to hurt others, but you can't spare people's feelings at the expense of you being bound by the same spirits that are binding them. Remember, Jezebel loves to manipulate others; they will play on your emotions if they see that you are uncomfortable rebuking them. Be loving and kind, but walk in your God-given authority. Additionally, do not ever try to usurp anyone's authority because if you do, you will walk in agreement with the Jezebel spirit and she'll be more than happy to come and live with (and in) you.

CHAPTER 9

Understanding Your Authority

Exodus 3:14 (ESV): *God said to Moses, " I AM WHO I AM." And he said, "Say this to the people of Israel: ' I AM has sent me to you.'"*
John 8:58 (ESV): *Jesus said to them, "Truly, truly, I say to you, before Abraham was, I am."*
Revelations 2:23 (ESV): *I am the Alpha and the Omega, the first and the last, the beginning and the end."*

Throughout the scriptures, you'll notice that God refers to Himself as "I Am." In the English context, this appears to be an incomplete sentence but, in truth, it's a complete statement. It encompasses who God is. Who is He?

- He is Love.
- He is the Truth.
- He is Alpha and Omega; the Beginning and the End.

When we come to know God as the "Great I Am," we are coming to know Him wholly. The word "I am" is usually followed up (in the English language) by a declarative word or a decree. For example, we can say, "I am blessed" or "I am sick." Either way, when we start a sentence with "I am", we are making a decree. When God referred to Himself as "I Am," He was making a decree. He's saying that He exists; there is no beginning or end to Him. He simply is. He's also making a blanket statement, whereas, He is confirming that His Word cannot return to Him void. What does this mean? Anything that "I Am" speaks is so. "I Am" said "Let there be light" and we know that light existed from the moment He uttered those words. As a matter of truth, He is Light (1 John 1:5). That's because He is the Great I AM; He is the Truth. We believe and receive this truth by faith.

Of course, we are created in the image of God. This doesn't necessarily mean that we physically "look" like Him; it means that we are miniature templates of Him. He has empowered us to decree a thing and whatever we decree, in faith, is established the moment we decree it. Google defines the word "decree" as: *an official order issued by a **legal** authority.*

We are legal authorities in the earth. Demons, however, are illegal and as such, they have no authority. For this reason, they have to borrow or steal our authority in order for them to operate. This is the reason they provoke men and women to perform witchcraft. They need the authority of the witches, wizards, and the warlocks to operate. They need conduits to channel their evil ways through, and because we are legal authorities, they seek to inhabit us so they can use our authority against the Kingdom of God.

One of the keys to deliverance from the Jezebel spirit, the Ahab spirit and any other demonic spirit that binds you is ... you simply need to know the Great I Am. You need to know the Word of God; that way, you can decree over yourself what God (the highest authority) has decreed over you. If you don't get to know the Great I Am, you will unleash word curses upon yourself or make ungodly decisions when the enemy comes and tags you with another identity. For example, the enemy will use a doctor to make a declaration over you. Understand this: the doctor cannot make a decree (legal statement) about you unless it lines up with what God has spoken over you. Google defines the word "declaration" as: *a formal or explicit statement or announcement.*

The doctor can make a statement in regards to you because you went into his office seeking a word from him, but his statement does not become your truth unless you receive it in the third dimension of your subconscious where truth resides. Because you have the legal right to make decrees involving yourself, the doctor's words cannot come to pass unless you stand in agreement with him (or her) and make that very same decree about yourself. For example, we've all heard stories about people suddenly being diagnosed with cancer, only to be told by their doctors that they've likely had the cancer for months or years. Nevertheless, they didn't have any symptoms of the cancer until the doctor made his or her declaration and the patient received what the doctor said. The person then made an *official decree* regarding himself or herself by saying, for example, "I have cancer." When those words left the individual's mouth, that person took the authority of the word "I," which is a legal reference to self, and coupled it up with an action word. The word "have" is a verb and what we've learned in English studies is that a verb is an action word. When placed behind the word "I," the word "have" points at the speaker. It is a decree from the speaker regarding himself or herself. Whatever word follows the word "have" is activated and will become the speaker's reality, especially if the speaker believes what he or she is saying. This is the nature of faith. One way to activate faith is by using words that reference self and coupling them with action words. When we have faith in God, we speak His Word over ourselves. When we have faith in science or people, we'll speak what they've spoken to us, and their words don't become our truths; they become our realities.

What's the difference between truth versus reality? Even though most people have attempted to make the word "truth" synonymous with the word "fact," the two are not one and the same. Truth is a supernatural statement that aligns with who God is and what God has spoken. It cannot be disproved, debunked, or made subject to another statement. Facts, however, are natural statements that have been established by mankind and decreed or declared to be truth in the natural realm. In short, the truth is a decree spoken by the highest legal authority (God), but a fact is a decree or a declaration spoken by a legal authority (mankind). When mankind (a legal authority) makes a decree or declaration that does not line up with the Word of God, his statement is rendered illegal, meaning it isn't truth; it is a lie. Additionally, the root word of "reality" is "real." Your reality is whatever is real to you; it is whatever you have legalized in your life.

Romans 3:4 (NIV): *Let God be true, and every human being a liar. As it is written: "So that you may be proved right when you speak and prevail when you judge."*

What does all this have to do with demonology and deliverance? It's simple. Demons manipulate people into believing lies about themselves. They do this because lies represent darkness, just as light represents truth. When a demon lies to a person, that demon is attempting to darken (sear) some area of the believer's belief system; that way, the demon itself can move in and control that particular area. At the same time, it can cause the legal authority (man or woman) to release decrees over themselves. Just like Jezebel sent out letters in Ahab's name, demons like to coerce believers into sending out official statements using their own voices. Why did Jezebel send out letters in Ahab's name? Because the king had the legal right to decree a thing, but the queen did not. Jezebel used Ahab's name to legalize a statement. This is the same thing that demons do. They get inside people and use them to decree things over themselves and others. By doing so, people legalize what God has already declared illegal. God is omnipotent, meaning, He's all powerful, but again, He has empowered us. This means that He has given us a measure of power and He has given us the freedom of will to exercise that power. Anytime, we use our power to legalize what God has declared illegal, we are guilty of practicing witchcraft.

Consider the United States government. Under federal laws, marijuana is illegal, but some states like California have legalized marijuana for medical purposes. Even though the state government is subject to the federal government, each state has the ability to create and enforce its own laws. The Tenth Amendment reads: *The powers not delegated to the United States by the Constitution, nor prohibited by it to the States, are reserved to the States respectively, or to the people.* This means that even though the federal government has supreme power, it cannot stop the state government from creating its own laws. The Supremacy Clause, which is Article VI of the Constitution, reads: *This Constitution, and the Laws of the United States which shall be made in pursuance thereof; and all treaties made, or which shall be made, under the authority of the United States, shall be the supreme law of the land; and the Judges in every State shall be bound thereby, any thing in the Constitution or laws of any state to the contrary notwithstanding.*

What does this mean? Even though state government has the ability to create and enforce its own laws, the federal government can override those laws. This is very similar to our God-given authority. Even though God is the Supreme Authority, He gives us the ability to bind (make illegal, arrest) and loose (legalize, allow) what comes in and goes out of our own lives. He is Sovereign, meaning, He is all-powerful. His Word overrides our words and His laws override our laws, but He allows us to be responsible for our own states (conditions) and states of mind (citizens). Our citizens are whatever thoughts and spirits we allow to live in us. When we receive the Holy Spirit, we allow the Sovereign Authority to override the laws that we have subject ourselves to, laws that once legalized demonic citizens to operate in our lives and hearts. This even allows our renewed minds to make citizens' arrests when any thought rises up that is contrary to the Word of God.

2 Corinthians 10:5-6 (KJV): *Casting down imaginations, and every high thing that exalteth itself against the knowledge of God, and bringing into captivity every thought to the obedience of Christ; And having in a readiness to revenge all disobedience, when your obedience is fulfilled.*

In the United States, if a person is arrested and found guilty under state laws, that person can appeal to the Supreme Court. It is up to the Supreme Court, however, if they will hear the case or not. If the Supreme Court decides to hear the case and the judge overrules the state's conviction, the Supreme Court's ruling will stand. That's because the Supreme Court is the federal court, whereas, state laws are under state jurisdiction. Again, this is similar to our relationship with God. Whatever states of mind we legalize in our lives can give place to the devil, meaning, it can give demons legal entry into our lives. When demons come in, they bind (place in bondage, arrest) the people they are inhabiting. When a person is too bound (usually psychotic and not of a sound mind), that person's demons will often speak when he or she is going through deliverance. They will say things like, "We have the legal right to be here because..." From there, they'll list the reasons they believe they are legal citizens residing within that person. This means that demons will act as their own lawyers. Sometimes, the bound person needs to renounce some things to disallow the demons from inhabiting them any further, but because they are extremely bound or possessed (unbelievers can be possessed), they cannot utter a word or offer the deliverance minister any assistance in freeing themselves. When this happens, the deliverance minister has to appeal to the Supreme Authority (God) for help. Sure, it is the finger of God that casts out demons, but we have to align our will with God's will to be free. When a person is possessed or they have extremely wicked demons that disallow them from thinking with a sound mind or speaking, that person more than likely won't align himself or herself with the Word of God. A demon may bind that person to a memory, for example, and that person may keep reliving a scene in his or her life. This means that even when the deliverance minister is present and speaking with them, they won't be in a conscious state to hear, see, or even acknowledge the words of the deliverance minister. They may keep speaking, for example, to a deceased relative and saying things like, "I didn't eat your peanut butter sandwich. I think Jason did." The person's will has been altered by a demonic spirit. To cast out such a demon, the deliverance minister needs to access the third level of the subconscious mind, but to do so, he first needs to fast because he has to go past the person's will. Since this is illegal, the deliverance minister needs to appeal to Jesus (the Supreme Authority) to override the person's will to get to the demonic entities. Consider the story of the man who had a host of demons call Legion.

Mark 5:1-13 (ESV): *They came to the other side of the sea, to the country of the Gerasenes. And when Jesus had stepped out of the boat, immediately there met him out of the tombs a man with an unclean spirit. He lived among the tombs. And no one could bind him anymore, not even with a chain, for he had often been bound with shackles and chains, but he wrenched the chains apart, and he broke the shackles in pieces. No one had the strength to subdue him. Night and day among the tombs and on the mountains he was always crying out and cutting himself with stones. And when he saw Jesus from afar, he ran and fell down before him. And crying out with a loud voice, he said, "What have you to do with me, Jesus, Son of the Most High God? I adjure you by God, do not torment me." For he was saying to him, "Come out of the man, you unclean spirit!" And Jesus asked him, "What is your name?" He replied, "My name is Legion, for we are many." And he begged him earnestly not to send them out of the country. Now a great herd of pigs was feeding there on the hillside,* *and they begged him, saying, "Send us to the pigs; let us enter them." So he gave them permission. And the unclean spirits came out and entered the pigs; and the herd, numbering about two thousand, rushed down the steep bank into the sea and drowned in the sea.*

This is a great example of a person whose will had been altered by demons. He had an entire government of demons operating in him and they'd pretty much taken over. Glory be to God, that man had an encounter with the Supreme Authority that day and was set free. Something likely happened in that man's bloodline that legalized the demons in his life, but Jesus came and overrode those bloodline curses. Another story to consider is the story of the young boy who had epilepsy. Jesus's disciples could not cast the demon out of the boy, so his father brought him to Jesus.

Mark 9:14-29 (ESV): *And when they came to the disciples, they saw a great crowd around them, and scribes arguing with them. And immediately all the crowd, when they saw him, were greatly amazed and ran up to him and greeted him. And he asked them, "What are you arguing about with them?" And someone from the crowd answered him, "Teacher, I brought my son to you, for he has a spirit that makes him mute. And whenever it seizes him, it throws him down, and he foams and grinds his teeth and becomes rigid. So I asked your disciples to cast it out,* *and they were not able." And he answered them, "O faithless generation, how long am I to be with you? How long am I to bear with you? Bring him to me." And they brought the boy to him. And when the spirit saw him, immediately it convulsed the boy, and he fell on the ground and rolled about, foaming at the mouth. And Jesus asked his father, "How long has this been happening to him?" And he said, "From childhood. And it has often cast him into fire and into water, to destroy him. But if you can do anything, have compassion on us and help us." And Jesus said to him, "'If you can'! All things are possible for one who believes." Immediately the father of the child cried out and said, "I believe; help my unbelief!" And when Jesus saw that a crowd came running together, he rebuked the unclean spirit, saying to it, "You mute and deaf spirit, I command you, come out of him and never enter him again." And after crying out and convulsing him terribly, it came out, and the boy was like a corpse, so that most of them said, "He is dead." But Jesus took him by the hand and lifted him up, and he arose. And when he had entered the house, his disciples asked him privately, "Why could we not cast it out?" And he said to them, "This kind cannot be driven out by anything but prayer."*

The King James version says that such a demon can only be driven out by prayer *and* fasting. Other translations leave out fasting but, in truth, fasting (on the part of the

person being delivered) is necessary to cast out such a demon. Adults were only allowed to fast back then, therefore, the boy who had the demon could not partake in fasting. The disciples had been casting out demons freely, but they came in contact with a high-ranking spirit that had altered the young boy's will. Since the boy could not fast, plus, the disciples could not legally go past the boy's will, they would have had to appeal to the Supreme Authority through fasting to cast out the spirit. Again, Jesus is the Supreme Authority, so He was able to override whatever demonic government was in place in that child's life and restore him back to a sound mind.
2 Timothy 1:7 (KJV): *For God hath not given us the spirit of fear; but of power, and of love, and of a sound mind.*

A legal authority can make decrees regarding the jurisdiction that authority has been given the power to cover. For example, a judge can decree that a person is guilty of a crime, but that judge can only make that decree in the courthouse and region that he or she has been granted the legal authority to officiate in. All the same, we have been given jurisdiction over our minds and our bodies, therefore, we have the right to establish decrees regarding ourselves. When we decree a thing, we establish it as our own personal truths. For example, if you say, "I am happy," you are pretty much calling happiness to yourself. You've made a decree, and if you believe what you've spoken, happiness will manifest itself for and in you because you have declared its presence in you as legal. If you decree, "I am poor," you are (at that moment) calling poverty to yourself because you have (at that moment) legalized poverty in your life. Even though your wallet and your bank account may be void of funds, the truth is ... you have the ability, as a believer, to call your reality a lie when it does not line up with what God has spoken over you. This means that you can override your "state of mind" laws with the Word of God. You can override facts with the truth. You can say, for example, "I am the lender and not the borrower; I am the head and not the tail. I come behind in no good thing. " Because this is the Word of God, it has to become the law in your life. Again, that is *if* you believe what you've said. Some people speak things that they do not believe and this makes their words declarations, not decrees. In other words, what they've spoken did not come from the third level of their subconscious, meaning, it was not released from their hearts, therefore, it was not released in authority. Because they released it from the realm of facts, they gave facts the ability to override truth in their lives. Remember, truth resides in the third level of the subconscious, but facts reside in the second level. In other words, whatever we receive as truth becomes the highest points of our personal governments. When we speak what we do not believe, we are speaking from the first level of our subconscious where things not necessarily believed nor received or housed. This means that what we are speaking is not coming from our hearts and therefore, has no legal standing in our lives.

Isaiah 29:13 (ESV): *And the Lord said: "Because this people draw near with their mouth and honor me with their lips, while their hearts are far from me, and their fear of me is a commandment taught by men.*

Understand this: there's a difference between speaking in authority versus speaking with an authoritative tone and demons know the difference. They will not leave when you are screaming words that you don't believe. Why not? Consider this: when a lawyer goes into a courtroom and pleads the case for one of her clients, that lawyer needs to know the law. If she does not know the law, the prosecutor can use the *same* law that would have set the person free to prosecute and get a guilty verdict for the person being prosecuted. The defense attorney needs to know the law to show why her client is either not guilty of the crime or is guilty of a lesser crime. She needs to be able to pick apart the same law that the prosecutor is using in a legalistic way and find a way to make that law defend the person being prosecuted. She can scream, speak in an authoritative tone, and even display confidence in her argument, but if she does not have the backing of the law, she will lose that case.

Devils do the same thing. They'll use the same scriptures that God sent forth to set us free in their attempts to bind us. For example, when Jesus was taken into the wilderness to be tempted by the devil, the devil was pretty much taking the Lord to court. He tried to use the scriptures to get what he wanted, but Jesus is the Word, therefore, He was able to disarm the enemy.

Matthew 4:1-11 (ESV): *Then Jesus was led up by the Spirit into the wilderness to be tempted by the devil. And after fasting forty days and forty nights, he was hungry. And the tempter came and said to him, "If you are the Son of God, command these stones to become loaves of bread." But he answered, "It is written,"'Man shall not live by bread alone, but by every word that comes from the mouth of God.'" Then the devil took him to the holy city and set him on the pinnacle of the temple and said to him, "If you are the Son of God, throw yourself down, for it is written, "'He will command his angels concerning you,' and "'On their hands they will bear you up, lest you strike your foot against a stone.'" Jesus said to him, "Again it is written, 'You shall not put the Lord your God to the test.'" Again, the devil took him to a very high mountain and showed him all the kingdoms of the world and their glory. And he said to him, "All these I will give you, if you will fall down and worship me." Then Jesus said to him, "Be gone, Satan! For it is written, "'You shall worship the Lord your God and him only shall you serve.'" Then the devil left him,* *and behold, angels came and were ministering to him.*

Even though Satan knew the Word, he could not override the Word. The wilderness scene between the Lord and Satan was nothing short of a courtroom where the enemy tried to use the same scriptures designed to set us free to stop the Word (Jesus Christ) from going forth. He tried to bind the Word with legalism! Because Jesus is the living Word of God, He was able to counter the words the enemy spoke with the Word. Satan took it even further. Jesus had been led into the wilderness by the Spirit of God, but the Bible tells us that after fasting 40 days and 40 nights that the Lord was hungry. This means that His flesh was weak, nevertheless, the Spirit was not.
Matthew 26:41 (ESV): *Watch and pray that you may not enter into temptation. The spirit indeed is willing, but the flesh is weak.*

When Jesus entered the "state" of hunger, Satan saw his opportunity. He then took the Lord out of the wilderness and onto the pinnacle of a temple. Why was this? Because Satan wanted to take the Lord out of the place that the Spirit of God had placed Him. Instead, he took Him onto the highest point of a religious temple. He was testing God with the spirit of religion! He thought that if he took the Lord out of the place where the Spirit had taken Him and placed Him at the top of a religious institution that he'd be able to argue his case with the Lord. In other words, he tried to take the Supreme Authority to the state courts because of the state (hunger) that He was in! When this didn't work, he took Him onto a high mountain and tested Him there. He realized that he'd lost in court, so the devil tried to offer Jesus a settlement offer. He showed him all the kingdoms of this world and their glory and then, he said, *"All these I will give you, if you will fall down and worship me."* Right then and there, the enemy went outside the scriptures and told the Lord to worship him. Before this statement, Satan was quoting scriptures and the Lord responded with scriptures, but when Satan tried to tempt Him, he'd offered the Lord a bribe. This illegal act allowed the Lord to cast Satan out of His presence. The point is: we have to know the Word to effectively cast the enemy out of our lives and our presence. When you speak the Word, but do not know the Word, meaning, there is no relationship between you and God, you have no legal recourse against the enemy. If you attempt to bind a demon while in this "state," demons will use your condition against you. Consider the sons of Sceva.

Acts 19:13-19 (ESV): *Then certain of the vagabond Jews, exorcists, took upon them to call over them which had evil spirits the name of the Lord Jesus, saying, We adjure you by Jesus whom Paul preacheth. And there were* *seven sons of one Sceva, a Jew, and chief of the priests, which did so. And the evil spirit answered and said, Jesus I know, and Paul I know; but who are ye? And the man in whom the evil spirit was leaped on them, and overcame them, and prevailed against them, so that they fled out of that house naked and wounded. And this was known to all the Jews and Greeks also dwelling at Ephesus; and fear fell on them all, and the name of the Lord Jesus was magnified. And many that believed came, and confessed, and shewed their deeds. Many of them also which used curious arts brought their books together, and burned them before all men: and they counted the price of them, and found it fifty thousand pieces of silver. So mightily grew the word of God and prevailed.*

What's interesting about the sons of Sceva is that they attempted to perform deliverance on a man without having faith in Jesus Christ. They said, "We adjure (command) you (the demon) by Jesus *who Paul preached about*. They did not reference Jesus as the Christ because they did not know or believe that He is the Son of God. This means they were unbelievers who likely had demons themselves, attempting to cast out demons. They had *no legal authority* over demons, so the demons (using the body of the man they possessed) attacked them and disrobed them. This disrobing was symbolic of them trying to cast out demons without a covering.

No individual guy said, "I command you" when referencing the evil spirits. Instead, the men trusted in their own numbers and said, "We command you." One thing you'll learn about God is that even though He loves unity, He despises when people trust in their own strength and their own numbers. That's why the Lord sent home more than 10,000 warriors and He only allowed Gideon to take 300 warriors into war with him against the Midianites (Judges 7). This is why Satan tempted David to count all of Israel, and when David did, the judgment of God fell on Israel (1 Chronicles 21). This is why God didn't allow David to fight Goliath while wearing armor made with man's hands (1 Samuel 17). In unity, there is no "we." There's only "I," meaning, the people are as one person (Genesis 11:6).

In the ministry of deliverance, you will rarely (if ever) hear a team of deliverance ministers saying to a demon, "We command you to come out of him." Instead, they will operate as a united front, and one will head up the deliverance. That deliverance minister will reference himself or herself and use his or her own authority. The minister will say, "I command you in the name of Jesus Christ to come out of him!" When this happens, the deliverance minister is activating the word "I" with the word "command." What he or she is saying is, "I issue a commandment (new law) by the legal authority granted to me through Jesus Christ that you must come out of him!" As believers, we have the right to sign Jesus's name to our decrees when they line up with God's Word. After all, Jesus gave us authority (jurisdiction, power) over unclean spirits.

Luke 10:19 (ESV): *Behold, I have given you authority to tread on serpents and scorpions, and over all the power of the enemy, and nothing shall hurt you.*

Demons are subject to the name of Christ Jesus, but when we use His name in the arena of deliverance, we must wear the helmet of salvation and yield the sword of the Spirit. We must also wear the breastplate of righteousness and secure it with the belt of truth. Additionally, we must protect ourselves with the shield of faith. Lastly, we must have our feet fitted with the gospel of peace. If you attempt to confront a demon without the helmet of salvation, you are attempting to confront it without a covering. It'll either attack or enter you and begin to oppress you. If you don't have the shield of faith, the enemy will throw darts (words and accusations) at you and those words will pierce you and cause you to need deliverance yourself. I've seen a few videos where deliverance ministers got offended because the demons said something about them that embarrassed them or hurt their feelings. In these videos, I noticed that the minister tends to get violent towards the person being delivered and will do things like ... pulling that person's hair or screaming angrily at the demon. This means that they lost focus on the demon and started attacking the person who's going through deliverance. The devil successfully got them in their flesh ... just where he wanted them! Of course, in the end, the person appears to be delivered (which is why they posted the video in the first place), but I suspect that the enemy simply found himself a new home in some of those cases and that new home was the minister, himself (or herself). If you are not wearing the breastplate of righteousness, you have no legal authority to cast anything out of the person you are attempting to deliver. Why is this? Because you have no authority over that person, but the Word of God does! In other words, the demons will come out at the sound of the Lord's name, but if you're not guarded, they'll enter or attack you. If you're not holding the sword of the Spirit, you will have many words, but there won't be any godly force available to carry out what you've spoken. If you're not wearing the belt of truth, the enemy will expose all of your lies and proceed to whip you with whatever belt you are wearing. Lastly, if you're not wearing shoes fitted with the gospel of peace, you will approach the enemy in the wrong state and just like he did the sons of Sceva, he'll overcome you (win his case), prevail against you (take authority over you) and send you running away naked (rip off your religious covering and cast you out).

When confronting the Jezebel spirit, the Ahab spirit or any other demonic spirit, we must approach the entity in the name of Jesus Christ. Since we are conduits, we are allowing the power of God to flow through us and that's why we reference ourselves during the deliverance. For example, we'll say things like, "I command you in the name of Jesus Christ" to come out of him." In this, we are partnering with the Lord to cast out demons. We are simply allowing Jesus Christ to work in and through us. Since the person being delivered is subject to the Word of God, just as demons are subject to the Word of God, deliverance will begin to take place if you simply trust God and you don't allow the devil to get you angry, prideful, or fearful. Demons love to incite negative emotions during deliverance; that way, the deliverance minister will start trusting in himself or herself and attempt to perform the deliverance without God. This would then allow the demons to do to the deliverance minister what the demons did to the sons of Sceva.

Next, we must remember to only decree over ourselves what God has decreed, and we should never "officiate" someone else's declaration about us when that declaration does not line up with what God said regarding us. We all have individual jurisdiction over ourselves, therefore, we get to decide what enters and exits our lives. We get to decide the "states of mind" that we live in.

Lastly, please note that saying that you don't have demons in you will not cause them to leave if they are, in fact, binding you. Instead, your statement will be rendered as a declaration and declarations (mere words) don't have the power to override decrees (legalized words). If you are in need of deliverance, understand that the demons found some legal way to enter you. They can live in darkness, so if you let darkness in, you gave them the right to live in you. During deliverance, demons often speak out of the person's mouth and say things like, "I have the legal right to be here, so I'm not coming out!" Demons almost always speak of their rights because they understand laws and authority. What they're saying is, "My presence here is legal ... and here's why!" From there, they'll proceed to tell the deliverance minister what legalizes their presence. In other words, they recognize believers as officers, so when they get caught behind the "will" of a person, they will show the deliverance minister what can best be described as their "driver's license." They'll show the minister why they believe they have the right to drive that person crazy. In one case where I was taking a woman through deliverance, the demons that were in her declared that they had rights to be in her. When I asked the demons what legal rights they had to her, they spoke and said that she'd been diagnosed with a mental illness by her doctor. She was given documents that declared her to be mentally ill. They tried to use this as their legal grounds to stay in her. The doctor declared something over the woman and she received his declaration and legalized his words in her life. Understand this: demons think like lawyers; they'll appeal any and every piece of evidence that you come after them with. Needless to say, I told the woman to renounce what was spoken over her and burn those papers. She needed to replace a decree she'd spoken over herself with the Word of God. In other words, she needed to establish a new law in her life; that way, the demons would be illegal and could be easily cast out. You have to take away Jezebel's rights to you, otherwise, the deliverance minister can cast her out, but she'll only find her way back in if she can find a legal right to inhabit you.

Your God-given authority is in your decree. Start decreeing over you what God has said about you. In other words, legalize the Word of God in your life; that way, anything you've received that is contrary to the Word will be overridden and declared illegal. When this happens, demons have no legal ground to stay in you and it will be a lot easier to cast them out and keep them out!

Once you do this, you can call them out by name or by function and they have no choice but to come out of you!

CHAPTER 10

Guard Your Heart

One of the spirits the Jezebel network likes to use is a spirit of witchcraft. One of the goals of the witchcraft spirit is to deceive believers. That's why Paul asked the church of Galatia in Galatians 3:1, *"You foolish Galatians! Who has bewitched you? Before your very eyes Jesus Christ was clearly portrayed as crucified."* Paul was pretty much saying that the church in question seemed to be under some type of spell.

One of the Greek words for "deceive" is "planaó" and it means:

> to cause to stray, to lead astray, lead aside from the rigid way.
> metaphorically, to lead away from the truth, to lead into error, to deceive.
> to wander or fall away from the true faith, of heretics.

(Reference: Thayer's Greek Lexicon/ Strongs NT 4105)

Paul was asking the Galatians to identify the person or

group who'd led them astray. He recognized that the people were not fully submitted to God because they were trying to go back under the Mosaic Law. Because he'd taught them, Paul knew that someone had been tampering with them. This is very similar to how a husband is with his wife. If the wife commits adultery, her husband may recognize that she's been tampered with. He recognizes this, of course, when he engages in sex with her or simply by her changed ways. The same is true for a father and his daughter. If a man's daughter enters a sexual relationship with someone, the father (if he's close to her) will recognize a change in her behavior. She'll become more distant and rebellious and when a father notices this behavior, he knows that someone has been with his daughter. Paul was serving as the apostle over the church of Galatia, therefore, like any good father in the faith, he knew that something was wrong. Someone had come along and taught the church a different doctrine than the one Paul taught them.

Jezebel loves to tamper with the people of God. That's why they can be found at the back of some church attempting to speak secretly to one of the members. They like to be "off record" so that they can bewitch the people of God through the use of seductive words and seducing spirits. They especially like to seduce God's prophets. Remember, the Bible tells the story of Jezebel having killed a large number of God's prophets, but Obadiah managed to hide 100 of them. I think most people would want to know how she managed to kill true prophets of God. Didn't God warn them; after all, they could hear from Him? The answer is ... more than likely, Jezebel seduced them into error. Once she got them out of the will of God, she slaughtered them. The ones who got away were hidden in caves, eating bread and drinking water daily. They sacrificed their carnal desires and this is how they managed to avoid Jezebel. This means that they had to give up the luxuries we so often take for granted in order to survive. The ones who could not or would not give up those luxuries found themselves at the edge of Jezebel's sword. This is why it is very important for prophets to not get too comfortable in a church, friendship, job, region, etc. This isn't to say that a prophet's life is unstable; it is to say that a prophet of God needs to be prepared to move if and when God says to move, otherwise, that prophet can find himself or herself at the mercy of Jezebel.

One of Jezebel's specialties in is distracting prophets with flesh. What does this mean? When a prophet undergoes an attack, Jezebel doesn't want the prophet to see the spirit behind the matter. She wants the prophet to focus on the person; that way, the prophet can enter unforgiveness, and bitterness can start setting up in the man or woman of God's heart. For example, in my years on social media, I've seen my fair share of men and women of God whose ministries suddenly seemed to be centered around people. Every time they write a post, preach a message or say anything relating to church, they are always talking about their enemies, false prophets, and everyone *they feel* should not have a platform. This doesn't mean that the prophet who's speaking this way is a false prophet. All too often, what has happened is the prophet got wounded and those wounds caused the man or woman of God to be distracted by personalities, rather than being focused on the spirit behind the matter.

Ephesians 6:1 (ESV): *For we do not wrestle against flesh and blood, but against the rulers, against the authorities, against the cosmic powers over this present darkness, against the spiritual forces of evil in the heavenly places.*

If we focus on the spirit behind the matter, we can bind that spirit and Jezebel knows this. So, anytime Jezebel attacks a person, she will often use a particular person in that person's life to carry out the attack. Why does she love to use the people we are familiar with? Because they have the most intimate access to us. The more intimate access a person has to your heart, the more damage that person can do. For example, I remember talking to a brother in Christ (Tony) when I was in a heavy battle with Mara. I was a babe in Christ back then, but I understood right from wrong.

I'd allowed hatred to enter my heart for Mara, and even though I tried to deny this fact, the evidence was in my words. I couldn't hear or say her name without getting angry. I'd convinced myself that she didn't deserve to live because of the wickedness of her heart. I realized my thinking patterns were wrong, so I began to pray about them. While talking with Tony, I spoke of that hatred in past tense, meaning, I testified about having "hated" Mara at some point. Little did I know, that hatred was still present. When I told Tony that I'd once hated Mara, he said to me, "That's because you took your eyes off that demon and started looking at the woman." He was right. In the beginning, I'd acknowledged that my war was against the spirits that were in Mara, but after a few years of persistent warfare, I saw Mara as the demon.

Another day came and I was boasting to my ex about Mara's attacks against our marriage being pointless. "I don't know why she keeps talking about me and trying to split us up," I said. "Can't she see by now that her attacks aren't working?" I laughed as I spewed out the venom that was in my heart, not realizing that at that point, I was snarling. I hated her and I needed deliverance. Almost immediately, the Lord addressed me. He said, "Satan wasn't trying to attack your marriage. His goal was to get you in unforgiveness and he succeeded." My heart broke right there. How did I not see the attack for what it was? How had I, as a woman of God, allowed myself to enter hatred? Regardless of how convicted and wicked I felt, I kept praying and asking God to set me free. I knew that I needed help because as much as I'd tried, I could not let go of that bitterness.

Because my heart was bitter, my views of the world became skewed. I couldn't watch too many television shows or movies about in-law interruptions in marriage without me screaming bitterly at the television set. "Leave his weak behind!" I'd yell. "He probably wears panties under that uniform!" My heart was sick and I couldn't hide it. Nevertheless, I prayed daily for help because I didn't know how to get free of that hatred, especially given the fact that Roger spoke with Mara every day and she would use almost every opportunity she had to speak evil of me.

When God delivered me from that hatred, I didn't experience a "feeling" of forgiveness, nor did I suddenly wake up and think, "I don't hate her anymore." Instead, He gave me understanding. He helped me to see that Mara was not well. She needed deliverance and the measure of force she'd used against my marriage represented the level of pain and hatred she had in her heart. Mara, the person, wasn't attacking me. The spirits in Mara were attacking me and they were using her pain and her hurt to propel themselves. Suddenly, I started feeling compassion towards Mara and I didn't want her to die and go to hell anymore. I wanted her to get saved, sanctified and filled with the Holy Spirit. God reminded me of how wicked I had once been. He'd forgiven me for my repeated transgressions and now, I was being given the opportunity to extend that love to someone else. I had been engaging in war when I should have been engaging in warfare. An effective warfare strategy should have been me binding and warring against the spirits in operation, all the while, extending love and forgiveness towards Mara.

I have since learned that love is best executed when it is unmatched. What does this mean? It means that love works best when you extend it to people who don't have it within them to give it back to you.
Matthew 5:43-48 (ESV): *"You have heard that it was said, 'You shall love your neighbor and hate your enemy.' But I say to you, Love your enemies and pray for those who persecute you, so that you may be sons of your Father who is in heaven. For he makes his sun rise on the*

evil and on the good, and sends rain on the just and on the unjust. For if you love those who love you, what reward do you have? Do not even the tax collectors do the same? And if you greet only your brothers, what more are you doing than others? Do not even the Gentiles do the same? You therefore must be perfect, as your heavenly Father is perfect."

Love is a powerful weapon against the enemy and that's why he works tirelessly to take it away from us. He finds us in our states of rebellion and couples us with rebellious people who have no desire to serve God. He then uses those people to wage war against the love in us. Sadly enough, many people (including prophets) have let bitterness consume their love. I almost did the same, so I understand how hard it is to hold on to love when you are engaging in daily warfare, but there is no excuse to let your love die. God told us to guard our hearts. In the top, innermost chamber of our hearts, we have the spirit of love. Satan can't destroy love, but he can cause us to reject it. This is how he battles the prophets of God. He attacks God's prophets in the arena of love.

How does one stop this attack?

In the Relationship Arena

First and foremost, you must stay fully submitted to

God. Follow the Word of God without fail. Next, you need to be submitted to a godly leader. Make sure the leader is someone God has assigned you to and not someone you've assigned to yourself. Thirdly, know your level of maturity. I got married both times when I was a baby Christian in need of some major deliverance. Because I saw that I was grown naturally, I thought I could marry who I wanted and do what I wanted. *I was wrong.* I came to understand that a child of God (especially a prophet) cannot and should not pick his or her own spouse. Why is this? We often pick spouses according to our maturity levels at any given time, and when we're immature, we'll choose immature spouses. This means that we can't blame them for being immature once we've matured! Additionally, if you meet someone who is cleaving to a family member in an unnatural way, do not enter a relationship with that person because you'll only be interfering. You will be the infamous "other woman" or the "other man" when coming between Jezebel and whomever it is that she has ahab'ed. Lastly, if you meet someone, you need to introduce that person to your pastor; that way, he or she can test the spirit if you're too immature or blinded by soul ties to test it yourself.

In the Church Arena

Don't get caught up in the traditions that are centered around church. Be fully led by the Spirit of God and only go where God sends you. A lot of God's people and prophets endure church hurt because they go to churches that they have not prayed about and they submit to leaders that God did not call them to serve! Just like with romantic relationships, it is easy to be misled by your emotions when choosing a church home. The best thing to do is let God choose for you, after all, you are not your own.

In the Friendship Arena

Let God choose your friends. I spent a lot of time after my failed marriage telling the friends who God had not assigned to my life how I was gonna avoid marrying another man who God had not assigned to my life. I was guarding my heart in one direction, all the while, leaving it wide open in the other direction.

In the Family Arena

God *never* said that we were supposed to sit with wicked, unrepentant family members and let them attack us in the name of love. The minute you got saved was the minute you received a new family. Every other family member has to be grafted into your relationship with God and not the other way around. When family members get saved and decide to follow God, they are your family, not through your natural blood, but through the blood of Christ Jesus. When family members do not want salvation, your only assignment is to pray for them. You can't open your house and your life to people who love their demons, even if those people are related to you! If you do, you will find yourself battling for your love time and time again, and because they have intimate access to you, it'll be easier for you to lose your love than it is for you to keep it.

Guard Your Heart

Proverbs 4:23 (ESV): *Keep your heart with all vigilance, for from it flow the springs of life.*

Everyone who has intimate access to you has access to your heart. This includes the people you listen to on the radio and the folks you watch on television. An unguarded heart is like a bank without vaults! You can't be casual in your dealings with random people. You need to pray about everyone in your life and everyone who attempts to enter your life. I found myself in many sinking ships that I called friendships because I'd had an emotional conversation with a person and confused our ability to relate to one another with us actually being spiritually related. Because of this, God had to deliver me from those ships before they sank and He had to deliver the people from those ships as well. Understand this: sometimes, two people can be in Christ Jesus, but still not be assigned to walk together. This is especially true when the uncrucified nature of one believer feeds the uncrucified nature of another believer. Sometimes, we meet people that we connect in the flesh with and confused those connections for God-appointed relationships when they are not.

Proverbs 4:23 tells us that the springs of life "flow" from the heart. This should put us in the mindset of a body of water. If you had a well on your property and it was the only source of water you had, you'd:

- Make sure the well wasn't near any sources that could contaminate it.
- Check the pipes often to ensure that they weren't rusting or corroding.
- Make sure the casing of your well extended the recommended distance above the land.
- Have your well inspected often.
- Have the pipes changed if they are stopped up or corroded.

We have to apply this same maintenance to our hearts to get and stay delivered. It is error to have a well installed and then, stopped guarding or testing it. For example, I have to conduct daily heart checks, especially when I'm offended. This is to ensure that my heart isn't clogged with unforgiveness and I haven't allowed bitterness to contaminate me. I do this by monitoring my thought patterns. If I have a day where I notice that most of my thought patterns are negative, I know to go and war for my mind. I have to start casting down thoughts and everything that is battling against my love. **2 Corinthians 10:3-6 (ESV):** *For though we walk in the flesh, we do not war after the flesh: (For the weapons of our warfare are not carnal, but mighty through God to the pulling down of strong holds;) Casting down imaginations, and every high thing that exalteth itself against the knowledge of God, and bringing into captivity every thought to the obedience of Christ; And having in a readiness to revenge all disobedience, when your obedience is fulfilled.*

If I can't cast the thought down, it simply means it has to be cast out. It means that I need to take myself through deliverance. So, I utilize my prayer time to start renouncing every ungodly thought pattern and binding every spirit that the Lord alerts me to. I then tell those spirits to leave and go into the abyss. Oftentimes, the response is I'll start yawning. This is common with deliverance. The truth is ... we need deliverance often and if we don't get it, the enemy will overwhelm us with negativity, hurt, pain and anger. Those things can become bitterness, rage and even murder. That's why it's important for us to guard our hearts, even after we've gone through deliverance. Deliverance is never a one-time event; it is a lifestyle!

WARFARE SCRIPTURES

"Submit yourselves therefore to God. Resist the devil, and he will flee from you."
James 4:7 (ESV)

"Be sober-minded; be watchful. Your adversary the devil prowls around like a roaring lion, seeking someone to devour. Resist him, firm in your faith, knowing that the same kinds of suffering are being experienced by your brotherhood throughout the world. And after you have suffered a little while, the God of all grace, who has called you to his eternal glory in Christ, will himself restore, confirm, strengthen, and establish you. To him be the dominion forever and ever. Amen."
1 Peter 5:8-11 (ESV)

Finally, be strong in the Lord and in the strength of his might. Put on the whole armor of God, that you may be able to stand against the schemes of the devil. For we do not wrestle against flesh and blood, but against the rulers, against the authorities, against the cosmic powers over this present darkness, against the spiritual forces of evil in the heavenly places. Therefore take up the whole armor of God, that you may be able to withstand in the evil day, and having done all, to stand firm. Stand therefore, having fastened on the belt of truth, and having put on the breastplate of righteousness, and, as shoes for your feet, having put on the readiness given by the gospel of peace. In all circumstances take up the shield of faith, with which you can extinguish all the flaming darts of the evil one; and take the helmet of salvation, and the sword of the Spirit, which is the word of God, praying at all times in the Spirit, with all prayer and supplication. To that end, keep alert with all perseverance, making supplication for all the saints, and also for me, that words may be given to me in opening my mouth boldly to proclaim the mystery of the gospel, for which I am an ambassador in chains, that I may declare it boldly, as I ought to speak."

Ephesians 6:10-20 (ESV)

"Then he said to me, "This is the word of the LORD to Zerubbabel: Not by might, nor by power, but by my Spirit, says the LORD of hosts."

Zechariah 4:6 (ESV)

"Behold, I have given you authority to tread on serpents and scorpions, and over all the power of the enemy, and nothing shall hurt you."

Luke 10:19 (ESV)

"Truly, I say to you, whatever you bind on earth shall be

bound in heaven, and whatever you loose on earth shall be loosed in heaven. Again I say to you, if two of you agree on earth about anything they ask, it will be done for them by my Father in heaven. For where two or three are gathered in my name, there am I among them."

Matthew 18:18-20 (ESV)

"You shall not fear them, for it is the LORD your God who fights for you.'"

Deuteronomy 3:22 (ESV)

"The LORD will cause your enemies who rise against you to be defeated before you. They shall come out against you one way and flee before you seven ways."

Deuteronomy 28:7 (ESV)

"No temptation has overtaken you that is not common to man. God is faithful, and he will not let you be tempted beyond your ability, but with the temptation he will also provide the way of escape, that you may be able to endure it."

1 Corinthians 10:13 (ESV)

"So Jesus said to the Jews who had believed him, 'If you abide in my word, you are truly my disciples, and you will know the truth, and the truth will set you free.'"

John 8:31-32 (ESV)

"What then shall we say to these things? If God is for us,

who can be against us?"
Romans 8:31 (ESV)

"Do not be overcome by evil, but overcome evil with good."
Romans 12:21 (ESV)

"Through you we push down our foes; through your name we tread down those who rise up against us."
Psalm 44:5 (ESV)

"And they have conquered him by the blood of the Lamb and by the word of their testimony, for they loved not their lives even unto death."
Revelations 12:11 (ESV)

"He gives power to the faint, and to him who has no might he increases strength. Even youths shall faint and be weary, and young men shall fall exhausted; but they who wait for the Lord shall renew their strength; they shall mount up with wings like eagles; they shall run and not be weary; they shall walk and not faint."
Isaiah 40:29-31 (ESV)

"Have I not commanded you? Be strong and courageous. Do not be frightened, and do not be dismayed, for the LORD your God is with you wherever you go."
Joshua 1:9 (ESV)

"One man of you puts to flight a thousand, since it is the LORD your God who fights for you, just as he promised you."

Joshua 23:10 (ESV)

"He who dwells in the shelter of the Most High will abide in the shadow of the Almighty. I will say to the Lord, "My refuge and my fortress, my God, in whom I trust." For he will deliver you from the snare of the fowler and from the deadly pestilence. He will cover you with his pinions, and under his wings you will find refuge; his faithfulness is a shield and buckler. You will not fear the terror of the night, nor the arrow that flies by day, nor the pestilence that stalks in darkness, nor the destruction that wastes at noonday. A thousand may fall at your side, ten thousand at your right hand, but it will not come near you. You will only look with your eyes and see the recompense of the wicked. Because you have made the Lord your dwelling place— the Most High, who is my refuge— no evil shall be allowed to befall you, no plague come near your tent. For he will command his angels concerning you to guard you in all your ways. On their hands they will bear you up, lest you strike your foot against a stone. You will tread on the lion and the adder; the young lion and the serpent you will trample underfoot.

"Because he holds fast to me in love, I will deliver him; I will protect him, because he knows my name. When he calls to me, I will answer him; I will be with him in trouble; I will rescue him and honor him. With long life I will satisfy him and show him my salvation."

Psalm 91:1-16 (ESV)

"And he said, "Listen, all Judah and inhabitants of Jerusalem and King Jehoshaphat: Thus says the LORD to you, 'Do not be afraid and do not be dismayed at this great horde, for the battle is not yours but God's."

2 Chronicles 20:15 (ESV)

"Little children, you are from God and have overcome them, for he who is in you is greater than he who is in the world."

1 John 4:4 (ESV)

"For though we walk in the flesh, we are not waging war according to the flesh. For the weapons of our warfare are not of the flesh but have divine power to destroy strongholds. We destroy arguments and every lofty opinion raised against the knowledge of God, and take every thought captive to obey Christ, being ready to punish every disobedience, when your obedience is complete."

2 Corinthians 3:10-6 (ESV)

Printed in Great Britain
by Amazon

58774376R00169